# WE FOUGHT BACK

## YOUNG RESISTERS
### OF THE HOLOCAUST
### BY ALLAN ZULLO

SCHOLASTIC INC.

TO MY GRANDSON DANNY MANAUSA,
WITH THE HOPE THAT WHEN HE FIGHTS BACK,
IT'S ALWAYS TO RIGHT A WRONG.
— A.Z.

About the back-cover photo: The Grynszpan group was among
the most notable of the 27 Jewish partisan units that operated
in Eastern Europe between 1942 and 1944. The Grynszpan unit
functioned as the protective force of the Jewish family camps that
had been set up in Poland's Parczew Forest. The Jewish unit
participated in attacks upon German police positions and army lines
of communication until the area was liberated in July 1944.

ISBN 978-0-545-38578-7

12 11 10 9 8                                    19 20/0

Printed in the U.S.A.                    40
First Scholastic printing, September 2012

Designed by Jennifer Rinaldi Windau

# ACKNOWLEDGMENTS

I WISH TO EXTEND my heartfelt gratitude to the former partisans featured in this book for their willingness to relive, in personal interviews with me, their stunning and emotional memories of their lives before, during, and after their experiences resisting the Nazis.

I am especially grateful for the cooperation and assistance of the Jewish Partisan Educational Foundation (jewishpartisans.org), especially JPEF's founding president and chairman emeritus, Paul Orbuch, who provided invaluable help. I also thank executive director Mitch Braff.

JPEF is a nonprofit organization that provides free educational materials to schools and cultural and faith groups about the history and life lessons of the Jewish partisans. The organization has documented the experiences of many partisans through recorded interviews, a collection of rare footage of them in action, their diaries, and Holocaust-era documents. As the world's largest online resource for information about Jewish partisans, JPEF's website offers short films, video clips of partisan interviews, curricula, study guides, an e-learning platform, biographies, interactive maps, and a page for virtual visitors to ask partisans questions. More than 5,000 educators around the world use the organization's materials.

I also wish to thank Varda Yoran, Lauren Feingold, Bea Hollander-Goldfein, and RuthAnn Moore.

# AUTHOR'S NOTE

You are about to read incredible true stories of teenage Jews who fought back against the Nazis during the Holocaust.

There is a mistaken impression among many people today that the six million Jews who were exterminated by the Nazis were led to their deaths without resisting. There was relatively little armed rebellion among the victims, mostly because the Nazis deviously hid their true intentions when they rounded up unarmed men, women, and children and shipped them off to death camps. For most Jews, there was no choice about whether or not to fight because they never had the chance to take up arms.

But by luck or by fate, thousands of Jews—many of them teenagers—slipped out of dehumanizing ghettos, concentration camps, and hiding places to join resisters known as partisans. Fighting primarily in eastern Europe, these brave men and women wreaked havoc on the Nazis through guerilla warfare and sabotage.

These warriors relished the opportunity to fight back. As Sonia Orbuch, a Polish-born partisan, explained, "If I was going to die, I was going to die as a fighter."

This book chronicles the experiences of Sonia and other young Jewish partisans. These accounts are based on the personal, lengthy interviews that I conducted with each former partisan featured in this book. Using real names, dates, and places, the stories are written as factual and truthful versions of their recollections, although the dialogue has been recreated for dramatic effect. (The words *Nazis* and *Germans* are used interchangeably, as are *Soviets*, *Russians*, and *Red Army*.)

Much of what you will read is disturbing because that's the way it really happened. But this book is also a celebration of the human spirit—of the will to overcome unspeakable horrors, the will to triumph over evil, the will to live. Despite facing overwhelming odds and unimaginable hardships, each person I interviewed fought back against a vastly superior force in terms of troop strength, arms, and equipment. In the most hopeless situations imaginable, these young partisans relied on their courage, faith, and smarts—and sometimes sheer luck—to strike back against the enemy.

Not only did they survive the Holocaust, but they grew up, married, and have enjoyed happy, productive lives. All of them have also turned their harrowing experiences into lessons for future generations by speaking at schools, churches, synagogues, conferences, and other gatherings. Most have written memoirs about their time as young partisans, which provided important material for this book.

I hope these stories will enlighten and inspire you, and help you understand how important it is to keep recalling the past . . . so no one ever forgets.

— Allan Zullo

# CONTENTS

# DEFIANCE AND RESISTANCE

LED BY DICTATOR ADOLF Hitler, the Nazi Party in Germany in the 1930s and 1940s believed that certain people—especially Jews—were inferior and didn't deserve to live. The Nazis were anti-Semitic, which means they hated the Jewish people, and planned to murder all nine million of them in Europe, in what was called Hitler's Final Solution.

As the German war machine invaded and occupied one country after another, the Nazis and their henchmen forced Jews to give up their jobs, homes, businesses, bank accounts, valuables, and rights. Jews had to wear the six-pointed Star of David, a symbol of Judaism, on their clothes to tell them apart from gentiles (non-Jews). They couldn't walk freely in the streets or do many of the things Europeans took for granted. Signs in theaters, cafés, restaurants, and other public places warned that Jews weren't allowed to enter. They were prohibited from possessing such items as telephones, shortwave radios, vacuum cleaners, cameras, and even certain kinds of food, like most meat, vegetables, and fruit.

To enforce these harsh laws, the police organization known as the Gestapo, and an elite army corps called the Waffen-SS, beat, tortured, and murdered Jews or sent them to inhumane prisons known as concentration camps. In countless villages, Jews were rounded up by the hundreds and executed, tumbling into mass graves that they had been forced to dig. This was known as the liquidation of a town.

The Nazis created ghettos—small walled-off areas inside cities, where Jews were made to live under unhealthy and crowded conditions. Every month, tens of thousands of Jews were deported to forced-labor camps or death camps where, unless they were useful to the Nazis, they were killed in gas chambers or murdered in other ways.

Most of the victims were tricked into believing they were being sent to decent work camps. They couldn't conceive that Germany—a civilized country that introduced the world to the beautiful music of Beethoven, Bach, and Brahms—was capable of murdering a whole race of people. As a result, Jews offered relatively little armed resistance at first.

But they did engage in other kinds of resistance. Some Jews smuggled children to safety, sneaked in food and medicine, and carried messages between the ghettos. Others forged documents so Jews could pass as gentiles. Jews in work camps sabotaged guns and other products that they were forced to make for the Germans. In defiance of Nazi laws, they held prayer services, taught children to read Hebrew, wrote poems and songs, and painted pictures to maintain their dignity, self-respect, and faith.

As the truth about mass exterminations slowly leaked out

to the world, some Jews, often through luck or fate, took up arms. An estimated 20,000 to 30,000 Jews—mostly teenagers and those in their twenties—escaped from concentration camps and ghettos to form or join organized guerilla-warfare groups made up of resisters known as partisans. Many were determined to stop the Nazis from killing more Jews. Others sought to avenge the murders of their loved ones.

The number of partisans mushroomed after Germany attacked the Soviet Union in June 1941, shattering an alliance in which each country had occupied half of Poland. The Germans marched on Moscow, capturing millions of Red Army (Soviet) soldiers. But many besieged soldiers escaped into the forests and swamps of Poland and Ukraine, where they formed partisan brigades, supported by the Red Army, to harass the Nazis.

Throughout much of German-occupied eastern Europe, Jews fought side by side with hundreds of thousands of non-Jewish partisans behind enemy lines. The brigades were made up of former POWs (prisoners of war), Soviet soldiers, and anti-Nazi peasants and farmers from such countries as Poland, Lithuania, Czechoslovakia (which today is split into the countries of the Czech Republic and Slovakia), and Belorussia (now known as Belarus). However, there were several all-Jewish groups, some that consisted solely of fighters, and others, like the Bielski Brigade, that included hundreds of men, women, and children under the protection of fighters.

Jews who had weapons and knew how to use them were welcomed into most partisan units. In many cases, unarmed Jews weren't allowed to join unless they first obtained a gun, which meant they usually had to steal one or kill the enemy for one. Some Jews, however, were accepted solely because they knew the local terrain and could act as scouts.

An estimated 10 percent of the partisans were women. Although some were fighters and scouts, most did support work, such as cooking for the members and caring for the wounded.

The partisans lacked troop strength, arms, ammunition, supplies, and equipment compared to the massive German forces. But these ragtag units possessed guile, bravery, survival skills, and knowledge of the forests, mountains, and swamps.

The partisans excelled in disrupting Nazi supply lines. They blew up troop trains, destroyed vital bridges, blocked major roads, and knocked down communication lines. They also sabotaged numerous enemy power plants and factories and triggered uprisings in ghettos and prison camps.

Most successful partisan missions occurred under cover of darkness and with the help of the region's farmers and peasants, who provided valuable information and supplies. Without assistance from the locals, most partisans never would have survived the war. But not all civilians cooperated, so the partisans sometimes had to beg, borrow, bribe, and steal to get the things they needed to live and fight.

Jewish partisans had a much tougher time than their non-Jewish comrades. Many local residents were vicious Nazi sympathizers willing to kill or capture any Jew. As a result, the Jewish partisans often resorted to force and threats to obtain critical supplies and information.

Adding to the danger for Jewish fighters, many partisans themselves were anti-Semitic and hated Jews almost as much as they did the Nazis. In some of the brigades, the Jewish fighters were treated badly—and even murdered for the slightest reason—by their comrades. Such units tolerated the Jews only because they were all fighting a common enemy. To protect themselves, many Jews in anti-Semitic partisan groups hid the fact that they were Jewish.

Most partisans lived in the woods under harsh conditions. They conducted ambushes and hit-and-run attacks and were constantly on the move. They never stayed in one place for long because thousands of heavily armed enemy troops swarmed in the forests hunting for them. With few permanent shelters, the partisans slept under trees and in dugouts to protect against miserable weeks of subzero temperatures and hip-deep snow as well as days of unbearable heat and torrential rain.

Because of the scarcity of medical supplies and the need to remain on the run, wounded partisans typically were left behind to fend for themselves, especially in the early days of the war. Their code required that they commit suicide to avoid capture. Enemy bullets, bombs, and mines weren't the only cause of death. Partisans also died from infection, disease, and exposure to the extreme weather conditions. Because of a constant shortage of food, there were times when they went hungry for days. Adding to their discomfort, their worn-out clothes harbored disease-carrying lice.

And still they fought.

Although most partisan activity took place in eastern Europe, partisan groups also worked with the local underground in occupied France, Belgium, Italy, and other western European countries.

When the war in Europe ended with Germany's surrender on May 8, 1945, the Holocaust had claimed the lives of six million Jews, including three million Polish Jews. Another five million non-Jewish civilians died at the hands of the Nazis.

The death toll would have been much higher had it not been for brave resisters like the thousands of Jewish partisans who, against all odds, courageously fought tyranny and oppression.

# "MY PARTISAN LIFE HAS BEGUN!"
# PAUL STRASSMANN

IT WAS PAUL STRASSMANN'S first mission as a partisan, and he could feel the excitement quivering in his body and the adrenaline flowing through his veins.

He was preparing to blow up a Nazi train.

Just a few days earlier he had joined a small, ragged-looking partisan unit headed by a one-handed Russian named Batko. Now Paul, the 15-year-old son of a wealthy merchant, was poised at the edge of a forest, waiting for the right moment to strike. His fingers nervously tapped the special leather pouch he was carrying. Inside the pouch, which was lined with soft cotton padding, were ten highly sensitive blasting caps, which were four-inch-long, pencil-thin copper tubes.

Soon the group heard a freight train chugging from the south. "It's moving slowly, which means it's pulling a heavy load," Batko whispered to his six fellow partisans. "I'm guessing from the sound of it that we have about nine minutes to mine the rail. Let's go."

The men crept out of the woods onto a firm path that

separated two freshly plowed 100-yard-wide muddy fields. After moving to a ditch at the bottom of the rail embankment, Paul heard the train coming closer. "We now have less than five minutes to set up," Batko said.

Two two-man teams spread out in opposite directions about 100 yards away to protect Paul, Batko, and another comrade, who were running up to the tracks. With the locomotive's headlights visible in the distance, Batko removed some of the stone ballast between the railroad ties and placed two eight-pound bricks of TNT under the rails. Paul then handed him a blasting cap, which he attached to the end of an ignition cord and inserted in the TNT. He taped the other end of the cord to another blasting cap on top of the rail. If the mine was set up correctly, the front wheel of the locomotive would strike the blasting cap, setting off the ignition cord, which would burn at a rate of one foot per second, until the other end ignited the other blasting cap, causing the TNT to explode under the heaviest part of the train—the tender carrying the water and coal—and pull the locomotive and other cars off the tracks.

When everything was set, the train was less than a minute away. "Done," said Batko. "Let's get out of here."

In the excitement of passing the caps, Paul failed to snap the lid to the pouch. When he jumped up to follow Batko, all of the remaining caps spilled on the ground. *What have I done?* thought Paul. He had been warned that the squad had no way of replacing these extremely scarce blasting caps.

While Batko scampered down the embankment, Paul frantically searched for the caps. By this time, the train was only about 100 yards away. *I've got to find them!* Suddenly lights from the engine illuminated enough of the roadbed so that Paul could see the copper cylinders. He quickly scooped them up and shoved them into his pocket. Then he grabbed his rifle and started running.

The train was now seconds away from blowing up. In his panic, Paul couldn't find the path between the two muddy fields. With no time to spare, he jumped into the muck and tried to flee for his life, but the mud was so thick he slogged only about 25 yards before he knew the train would reach the TNT. All he could do was dive into the muck and hope for the best.

Just then the night lit up, and the ground shook in an ear-shattering explosion. Pieces of metal whizzed past his head and smacked into the mud. Although Paul wasn't hit by flying debris, he was slightly singed by the hot water that rained from the tender's wrecked steam boiler. Turning his head, he saw the front of the train slowly roll off the tracks in his direction. He heard the screams and shouts of soldiers and the crunching of metal as cars jammed against the tangled mass of already derailed cars.

Paul got up and plodded through the mud as fast as he could, which wasn't fast at all. The area lit up again, this time with a flare fired from the rear of the train. Then tracer bullets (which leave a lighted trail) from a machine gun raked the field and the edge of the forest. Terrified because this was his first experience under fire, Paul flattened himself in the muck. When the flare burned out, he began moving until another flare was shot. Once again he dove into the mud. The enemy continued to fire tracer bullets across both fields and into the forest. Fortunately, Paul was so smeared with muck that he was well camouflaged and looked like a lump of mud to the machine gunner.

Paul finally made it out of the field and into the forest, where he joined up with the others, who had fled without any casualties. Everyone was ecstatic over the damage they had inflicted on the enemy train.

Before heading back to the camp, Batko checked the readiness of the partisans' weapons in case they would face an ambush. Once he was satisfied everything was in order, he whipped out his revolver, aimed it at Paul, and declared, "Now let's get rid of the Jewish kid for losing the blasting caps."

Paul grew up with his older sister, Ella, in one of the most prosperous Jewish families in Trenčín, Czechoslovakia (now Slovakia). His father, Adolf, a former army officer, and his mother, Franci, owned and operated a flourishing wholesale food and agricultural products business. Because of Paul's tendency to pull pranks and get into trouble, his mother nicknamed him Spacek, taken from the Slovak word for a bird with a reputation for being daring, curious, and annoying.

Unaware of the war clouds building over Europe, Paul and his pals played cops and robbers in an old crumbling fortress on the steep rocky hill overlooking the town. Each "cop" wore a blue cloth ribbon on his right arm, each "robber" a red ribbon on his left arm. To "kill" the enemy, one had to rip off the other's ribbon. In the summer they also swam in the Váh River, despite its dangerous rapids, sharp rocks, and raw sewage.

Believing that Jews faced grave danger by Adolf Hitler's rise to power in Germany, Paul's parents secretly planned for the family to leave Czechoslovakia. They had been saving money, which Franci kept in a metal cigar box on the floor behind a radiator. Once they made the decision to emigrate, she retrieved the box. But when they opened it, they were stunned to discover that all the paper money was charred and crumbled to the touch. It was an unfortunate mishap. The last time Franci had put money in the metal box, she had slipped it behind the radiator as always, expecting it to end up on the floor. But the box had accidentally lodged between the radiator fins, causing it to heat up and act like an oven, which destroyed the money. Although Adolf was a stern man, he never scolded Franci or blamed her for ruining their plans to flee.

At the end of 1939, about eight months after Czechoslovakia fell under the control of the Nazis, the Strassmanns' business and house were taken away from them. Adolf was forced to work as a poorly paid bookkeeper for the company that he had created.

The family was ordered to move into a small two-room apartment near the Lutheran church. When the Jewish school was closed down, Adolf brought in private tutors so Paul and Ella could continue their education.

Being forced to wear the yellow star in a small town where most people knew one another became a source of humiliation. Anti-Semitic hooligans enjoyed mugging and harassing Jews, who were forbidden by law from hitting back. The Hlinka Guard, a Czech militia of Nazi sympathizers, looked for any excuse to beat or arrest Jews. Paul and his buddies were seldom beaten up because they were members of a militant Jewish youth group and always went together as an organized pack. Sometimes they even fought back.

With every month, the number of Jews who were deported increased. Before conditions deteriorated further for the Strassmanns, Adolf reached an agreement with a cleric of the Lutheran Church to convert the family to Christianity and baptize them in the faith. So six months after Paul's bar mitzvah (a coming-of-age ceremony for Jewish 13-year-olds), the Strassmanns became Lutheran, but in name only. It was just a way of trying to save their lives.

Within weeks, they each received a special white card that shielded them from deportation. This protection extended to Paul's grandparents as well. Being "Christian" meant they didn't have to wear the yellow star anymore. But all other restrictive laws against Jews still applied to the Strassmanns.

By 1943 Paul and his family were forced to move again, this time into the town's slum district, right next to the train tracks. Much of his time was spent scrounging for food and avoiding the penalties for violating the many rules that Jews had to follow. His sister, Ella, who was 18, obtained forged identity papers and found a job in the big city of Bratislava, where she hoped to avoid Nazi persecution.

The following year, the Strassmanns were buoyed by news that the German army had suffered a series of defeats in Russia at the hands of the Soviet army. As a major in the Czech army reserve, Adolf was aware that if the Germans were forced to retreat through his country, they would kill as many Jews as possible because "dead men can't ask for justice or demand the return of their stolen property." Hope rested on the Slovak National Uprising, a resistance movement launched on August 28, 1944, to drive the Nazis and their sympathizers out of Czechoslovakia.

Three nights later, a Gestapo officer and his henchmen came to the Strassmann home and took away Paul's father and his grandfather Dedko. The Gestapo wanted to seize Paul, too, even though he was only fifteen. But by sheer luck, he was spending the night with a friend.

After learning of the arrests, Paul managed to contain his shock and fear by following a plan set up earlier by his father in case of an emergency. Paul ran to the home of a trusted employee of Adolf's, who lived on the other side of the Váh River. Meanwhile, his mother went into hiding in Trenčín at a friend's house.

Paul stayed in the attic of the employee's home for two nights and hid during the daylight in the bushes along the riverbank while Nazis searched for Jews. However, the employee's wife panicked when the Gestapo announced that if they found any partisans, army deserters, or any Jews hiding in a home, everyone—including the owners of the house—would be executed. She made it clear she didn't want Paul hiding in her home anymore.

While sitting on the riverbank eating a sandwich and two peaches that the woman had given him, Paul pondered his fate, wondering what he should do next. It all became clear after he heard short bursts of machine-gun fire coming from Inovec Mountain, about 20 miles away. It sounded like a skirmish between the Germans and the partisans. To Paul, it was music to his ears. *I'm not going to hide anymore,* he told himself. *I'll go to where the war is being fought and become a hero as a partisan.*

To get there, he needed to cross the river, but he couldn't use the bridge because it was guarded. He couldn't swim across because on the other side was Trenčín, where he would be recognized. His only option was to escape down the river. Wearing shorts, a T-shirt, socks, and sandals, he put a bag of his belongings on top of his head and secured it with his belt, which he strapped under his chin. Then he grabbed a large branch for cover and plunged into the flowing river.

Because he often had played in the Váh, he knew how to float with the current and avoid the exposed sharp rocks in the rapids. Paul drifted for about an hour until he was safely out of range of any possible observers. The swim was refreshing and took his mind off the fate of his family.

After emerging from the river, he walked four hours to the village of Selec, where a family friend gave him a pair of pants and a cloth jacket. Then Paul headed for Inovec Mountain. Over the previous few years, he had learned how to blend into the landscape: Never walk on a road. Travel on cow paths behind village barns. Don't talk to strangers. Don't give your name to anyone. Never offer explanations even if asked. Don't pick somebody's fruit without permission. Drink plenty of water, but only from a mountain stream. If confronted by authority, act stupid and confused.

That evening, Paul reached the cottage of a gamekeeper who knew his father from the military. After getting a good night's sleep, Paul was given a thick slab of bacon, bread, and prunes and told to be careful because the area was crawling with armed members of the Hlinka Guard.

As Paul headed into the woods, his spirits were up because he could hear occasional gunfire from partisans not too far away. He soon encountered a group of lightly armed Slovak soldiers, who laughed at him when he asked to join them. Although he was fit and athletic, they wanted nothing to do with an unarmed 15-year-old. One of the soldiers offered him a grenade and said, "I'll give this to you on one condition—that you get out of our sight." Paul took it and left.

Later in the day, he met seven scraggly partisans whose leader, a foul-mouthed Russian named Batko, agreed to let Paul join on a tryout basis only because the lad boasted that he knew all the mountain trails—which was only half true. Paul acted as their unarmed guide for the next two days and impressed Batko enough to be made an official partisan and given a weapon.

After a mandatory drink of gut-searing, home-brewed

*slivovice* (plum brandy), Paul was inducted into Batko's Miners—the nickname for the unit assigned to blow up railroad lines. Paul was incredibly happy. *I'm finally in the company of armed men who are killing Germans and Hlinka guardsmen. My partisan life has begun!*

He had discovered that his brashness and fearlessness made up for the fact that he was so young and had never actually fired a weapon. He was given a carbine, 128 rounds, and two grenades. Into the wooden butt of his bolt-action rifle, he carved *pomsta*—the Slovak word for *vengeance*.

As the youngest member and only Jew in the unit, Paul was welcomed by his comrades who, unlike many members of other partisan groups, were not anti-Semitic.

Batko was a former Soviet soldier who, under orders from the partisan command in Kiev, Russia, parachuted into the Czech mountains to form a partisan unit. He had lost his left hand in combat or an accidental explosion while setting a land mine; no one was quite sure, and he wouldn't talk about it. Batko was a member of a handpicked group of special-forces soldiers whose sole purpose was to blow up enemy trains on the 120-mile-long main railroad line between Bratislava and Žilina.

The number-two man on the partisan squad was nicknamed Tato, a Slovak term for *father*. He was a gray-haired former machinist who had served in the Spanish civil war. He seldom spoke, but when he did, everybody listened, including his son, Michael, another member of the group. Other comrades included Milos, an engineering student from Moravia; Ivanko, who claimed to have escaped from a German concentration camp; Liška (Slovak for *little fox*), a local farmer who, despite his short size, was strong enough to carry heavy weaponry; and the red-haired Ivanov, a recently parachuted Soviet radio operator.

Batko was the only one in the group who had an automatic weapon—a Russian PPS with a round magazine that held 72 bullets. The other men were armed with World War I six-shooters, standard-issue Slovak army rifles, and hand grenades.

On Paul's first mission to derail a train, he led the group through the mountain forest in "open fire" territory, which meant the Germans and the Hlinka Guard could shoot anybody on sight. Because he knew the area, he was the designated point man and walked 100 yards ahead of the others. He understood that he likely would be the first one spotted by the enemy, and likely the first one killed.

In addition to his rifle and hand grenades, he carried leather pouches with ammunition clips, a backpack with food, and half of a standard army-issue tent. The squad took turns carrying the knapsacks that contained the explosives. On the second night of their trek, they reached the strategic railroad line near the village of Opatova.

Everything went smoothly for Paul until he momentarily lost the blasting caps and then, after the train blew up, had to scramble through the muck under fire. When he rejoined the rest of his group, he was elated because he had helped pull off a successful mission. But in a split second, his joy turned to despair when Batko aimed his gun at him and hissed, "Now let's get rid of the Jewish kid for losing the blasting caps."

Paul gasped. "B-b-but I didn't lose them." He stuck his hands in his pockets and pulled out a fistful of the copper cylinders. With gasps of alarm, the rest of the men backed away. Paul forgot that if he had squeezed the caps even slightly or had fallen on hard ground with them in his pocket, they would have exploded with enough force to kill him and injure anyone next to him. But they hadn't blown up while he was running from the railroad tracks because he kept falling into soft muck.

Batko smiled at Paul and put his gun away.

"He was only joking," one of the partisans whispered to Paul. "But that's only because you retrieved all the caps." Then he winked.

Over the next few months, Batko's Miners executed their missions at night, stayed out of villages, relocated their campsite every few days, and avoided firefights whenever possible. Paul was so occupied with trying to survive and carry out his assignments that he spent little time dwelling on the fate of his family.

He ate relatively well, mostly spiced pork stew with beans, cabbage, and potatoes, all generously flavored with paprika. Whenever he was at a major partisan base, he traded his rations of alcohol and cigarettes—neither of which he liked—for extra portions of bread and other food. After seeing hungry men willing to trade life-sustaining food to satisfy their addiction to cigarettes, Paul promised himself he would never smoke.

On Saturday everybody shaved. Being only 15, Paul had few whiskers, a fact that Batko used for a little good-natured teasing. "You have a sorry excuse for a beard," Batko told him. "But since you'll probably be killed anyway, you might as well look presentable, so go ahead and shave."

Batko's Miners kept moving north along the railroad line, looking for places where the tracks were close to a forest so that they could attempt another derailment and use the woods for cover. As time passed, the raids became more difficult because the Germans placed a machine-gun squad on a flat car ahead of each locomotive. The enemy also deployed rapid-response SS troops to hunt the partisans after attacks on the rail lines.

Between missions, Batko taught Paul how to survive an

attack. "In bad light, the enemy first recognizes only moving objects," Batko explained. "They rake the area with machine-gun fire, hoping to get us sufficiently scared to start running. If we do run, we become more easily identifiable targets. So don't move at night or in dusk when you're under fire. Move only after the enemy believes that we've disappeared."

For Paul it required incredible willpower not to flee whenever he and his comrades encountered overwhelming firepower.

Life for Paul and his fellow partisans soon turned into a series of setbacks. The Slovak National Uprising was crushed within two months of its start, allowing the Nazis to put more resources—such as the Hlinka Guard and German loyalists in the Slovak army—into attacks against the partisans. "Police action groups," made up of former Russian soldiers who had joined the Nazi cause, spread out into the countryside, burning villages, torturing peasants, and murdering Jews. But their specialty was hunting down partisans in remote places where regular German troops seldom went. Experienced, well-equipped commando raiders relied on local intelligence from informers who either gave information willingly or under torture.

When winter arrived—the most brutal in a decade—Paul found it difficult to stand guard as a sentry at night. He had to remain still, swiveling only his head because the

SS had snipers who could spot movement against snow illuminated only by starlight. But in the bone-numbing cold, it was virtually impossible for sentries not to stomp their feet and hop around to keep warm. So when Paul stood guard on moonlit nights, he always positioned himself within a shadow.

By early November, Batko's Miners were sick and physically exhausted. They hadn't washed for days and had picked up lice and fleas. Paul was miserable. Like his comrades, he suffered infections on his feet, which made walking increasingly painful. He couldn't hold down food rations of bread and fried bacon. For several weeks, he wore half a coat because part of it was burned while he slept too close to a campfire.

Casualties mounted. Tato and Milos suffered bad wounds in an ambush and were left behind in a village to either recover or die. Paul never learned how they fared.

Then came a demoralizing casualty. While hiking on a road near the village of Zavada, the partisans were caught by surprise when a truck approached from a curve. They all dove for cover except Batko. He kept walking calmly in the center of the road, resting his weapon over his handless left arm, and aiming at the vehicle until he could identify it as friend or foe.

From his vantage point, Paul could see a Nazi machine

gunner on top of the truck firing at Batko. Rather than flee, Batko broke into a dead run toward the vehicle, trying to kill the driver and machine gunner. Instead, it was Batko who was killed. After Paul and his comrades engaged in a brief firefight with the Germans, the partisans fled into the woods. Following the general rule of partisan warfare, they did not return for Batko's bullet-ridden body.

"Why didn't Batko duck for cover?" Paul asked a fellow partisan.

"Who knows?" came the reply. "He took risks. He either thought he was invincible, or he was trying to buy some time for the rest of us to get away."

*Lord, if I get out of this alive, I promise to grow up a good man,* Paul prayed.

Escaping from ambushes and mortar attacks over the next few weeks, the group headed for the safety of a large partisan base atop Čierny Vrch Mountain. Stragglers and men of questionable background who showed up were not allowed to stay. Neither were several Jewish families who came seeking protection by the partisans—a decision that pained Paul greatly. He assumed that, left to fend for themselves, those families perished.

During the partisans' monthlong stay on Čierny Vrch, the original unit of Batko's Miners was broken up. Paul was assigned to a group that went on weekly sorties to obtain food in the valley. It took most of a day just to go down the mountain and confirm that it was safe to enter a village. Another day or two was spent collecting the food, which usually included butchering a hog or sheep into quarters. Then the squad needed a day to lug the supplies up the steep icy slopes. Throughout each mission, the partisans were under continuous threat of ambush.

Late in November, the partisans were roused from sleep in the middle of the night and ordered to abandon their dugouts because an attack was expected at any moment. They packed whatever supplies they could carry and marched in a single column in hip-deep snow. The sick and wounded at the back of the pack had to follow as best they could or die.

For 20 straight, grueling hours, the partisans, now numbering in the hundreds, hiked over two mountain ranges. Shivering and fatigued as night settled in, Paul was somewhere in the middle of the column when automatic-weapons fire erupted in front of him. "Ambush!" Beyond the muzzle flashes, he saw moving figures in white camouflage—German forces specializing in winter warfare. *I can't believe they're attacking us at the top of a mountain at night,* he thought.

Acting instinctively, Paul clutched his rifle and rolled down a steep slope, losing much of what he carried in his backpack, including spare hand grenades, food, and half of a canvas tent. He slid about 100 feet until a tree stopped him. Above him, he heard wild shooting and shouting.

In a few minutes another partisan from Trenčín, named Hatlancik, skidded into Paul. "We've been ambushed by SS troops," said Hatlancik. "They're speaking Russian and pretending to be our comrades. Do you hear those orders for us to get back to the ridge and rejoin the march? Don't do it. It's a trap. Anyone who follows those fake orders gets shot."

The calls to come back were punctuated by spotty small-arms fire, which convinced Paul that returning to the ridge would be a deadly mistake. So he and Hatlancik worked their way down until they reached a brook in a ravine. On the opposite side, they faced another steep slope. Shooting was coming from all sides except the direction in front of them. The pair plunged into the ice-cold, waist-deep water and waded across. By the time they climbed to the top of the next slope, Paul's teeth were chattering so much that he had a hard time walking or even thinking.

Only a few partisans, like Paul and Hatlancik, had managed to escape the ambush. The survivors reassembled at the countryside's few remaining shelters, which were nothing more than farmers' hay sheds that hadn't yet been torched by the enemy. Because decaying hay produces heat, the partisans were able to warm themselves up. They couldn't depend on the local friendly peasants anymore for shelter because the villages were now crawling with members of the Hlinka Guard and informers.

The best hope of surviving was to reach the front of the advancing Russian army. That meant the partisans had to trek over several more mountain ranges in fierce winter weather in a difficult journey that, including stays at various safe places, would take nearly three months. They began walking east along mountain logging trails strewn with the bodies of many dead partisans as well as discarded equipment and gear from previous retreats and ambushes. Like his comrades, Paul was wet, hungry, shivering, and exhausted. His shoes were full of holes, and in place of socks, he wrapped each leg and foot with strips of linen. These improvised socks kept slipping while he hiked, creating sores wherever the cloth edges rubbed against his skin. Soon most of the skin below his knees was raw and infected. Fortunately, he had some sulfa powder to keep the painful condition from getting worse.

Paul also was suffering a high fever from a lung infection called pleurisy. Because the fever fogged his brain, he hiked without much awareness of his surroundings except to follow the backpack in front of him. Although he was still lugging his rifle, he didn't have the strength to load, aim, and fire it with any accuracy.

Only about half of the men who had started the march

arrived at their final destination. Many just gave up and wandered off or plopped down for a rest. Some fell asleep from exhaustion and froze to death. Others hiked to the nearest village and gave themselves up. Such choices were unacceptable to Paul.

To prevent his mind from drifting into despair or his legs from buckling, he created a dreamlike fantasy, visualizing the perfect life after the war. His brain kept generating movielike images of him walking on the streets of a great city with gleaming skyscrapers, riding in fancy cars, visiting lush gardens, and relaxing in front of a beautiful house. He pictured himself at a drafting table, working as a highly successful engineer, his childhood dream. Paul was mentally strong enough to call up any pleasant scene he wanted to imagine.

One of his fantasies became so real to him that he talked out loud as if he were actually there. When comrades asked what he was babbling about, he said in his feverish state, "I am on my way to America." They laughed and shook their heads. But had they understood Paul's steely resolve and will to live, they would have known this wasn't just some gibberish or a wild fantasy.

No, it was a dream he wouldn't let die. Nurturing his dream kept him alive throughout the darkest of days as a teenage partisan . . . until ultimately that dream came true.

Paul and his comrades finally reached an area of Czechoslovakia that had been liberated by the Soviet military. After he was diagnosed with advanced pleurisy, he was taken to a fancy hotel that had been converted into a hospital for wounded soldiers and sick partisans. For Paul, it was heaven to sleep in a bed with clean sheets and to savor an unlimited supply of bread and jam and soak in hot running water.

In spring 1945, Paul was given the rank of corporal in the Czechoslovakian army even though he was only 16 years old. He was ordered to go to the city of Bratislava to serve as bodyguard to a colonel in the military police. On his way, he stopped in his hometown of Trenčín for only one day. Despite months of daydreaming of revenge, he saw no point in settling any scores with the anti-Semites who had harassed him before he became a partisan. But he allowed himself the smug satisfaction of strutting around the main square in his new army uniform and seeing the fear in their eyes as they worried that he'd seek vengeance.

After serving in the army for three months, Paul received a discharge and returned to Trenčín, where he was reunited with his sister, Ella, who had barely survived in a slave labor camp. She told Paul that less than two months after she had left Trenčín for Bratislava, she was betrayed by someone who recognized her on the street and informed the police. Ella was forced to work in a factory that salvaged parts from downed war planes. While at Ravensbrück, the notorious women's concentration camp in Germany, Ella briefly saw their mother, Franci, who later died of typhus in 1945, shortly before the end of the war.

Paul and Ella learned that after their father, Adolf, was seized, he was taken to the Sachsenhausen concentration camp in Germany. Just days before the area was liberated, 33,000 prisoners were forced on a death march without food, water, or shelter. Thousands died or were shot because they were too weak to walk. Adolf was one of them. Paul and Ella also learned that their deported grandparents perished in the infamous death camp of Auschwitz.

Ella married her teenage sweetheart and together they raised two children in Trenčín, a town she never left again.

Paul wanted to start a new life in America, where he wouldn't be haunted daily by the people and places that reminded him of the war. So in 1948, at the age of 19, he arrived in New York with $26 in his pocket and soon got a job selling socks at a department store. In 1953, a year after he became an American citizen, Paul graduated from New York's tuition-free Cooper Union *with an engineering degree. He then worked his way through Massachusetts Institute of Technology, earning a master's degree in industrial management.*

*From 1962 to 2003, Paul held positions as an information systems executive for General Foods, Kraft, Xerox, the Department of Defense, and NASA. Following an academic appointment as adjunct professor at the United States Military Academy at West Point, he became a distinguished professor of information sciences at George Mason School of Information Technology and Engineering. In 1993 he received the Defense Medal for Distinguished Public Service, the Defense Department's highest civilian recognition. In 2003 he was honored as recipient of the NASA Exceptional Service Medal.*

*Paul and his wife, Mona, who live in New Canaan, Connecticut, raised four children and have seven grandchildren.*

*"If I learned one thing from my experience as a partisan," says Paul, "it's never give up."*

You can find more information about Paul Strassmann's life as a young partisan in his book *My March to Liberation: A Jewish Boy's Story of Partizan Warfare* (George Mason University Press).

# "IF I DIE, I'LL TAKE SOME GERMANS WITH ME"
# SELIM SZNYCER

HOME FOR TEENAGER SELIM Sznycer and four other Jews was a hand-dug, well-camouflaged hole deep in a forest teeming with danger. If they had any hope of fighting as partisans, they first needed to survive the bitter winter in their underground dwelling while remaining hidden from a relentless enemy on the prowl.

Selim and his older brother, Musio, had met their comrades in the woods of eastern Poland, all having fled their homes to escape ongoing massacres by German soldiers and Nazi sympathizers. Although the five were unarmed, they shared the same goal: to fight back. But that had to wait. Survival until the spring was their top priority.

After building a temporary hut out of twigs, they set out to construct their *zemlianka*, an underground shelter. Because they had no money to buy tools, they sneaked into barns and stole hammers, shovels, axes, saws, and buckets. Selim didn't feel guilty about the thefts—not when it came to survival; not when it came to all the terrors they had survived just to get this far.

They dug a pit 7 feet deep, 14 feet wide, and 20 feet long. Next, they chopped down pine trees, stripped off the branches, and lined the sides of the pit with logs. After hammering four wooden posts on the corners, the young men put up two 20-foot-long parallel beams. They made their roof out of thinner logs packed with moss for waterproofing and topped by dirt, grass, and a few small trees. They cut a small 2-foot-by-2-foot entrance and dug a 4-foot-deep pit outside the opening. To enter the *zemlianka*, they had to jump into the pit and crawl backward into the dugout on their belly. A small tree that they moved to get in and out was placed in the pit to disguise the entrance.

The back third of the *zemlianka* was used for storing potatoes, the middle third for sleeping on log bunks, and the forward third for dining and cooking on a small wood-burning stove they had stolen.

For food, they walked miles to villages, where they begged for things to eat or snatched potatoes from farmhouse cellars. But the group needed more provisions to make it through the long winter. That's when Selim came up with a bold idea. He cut off the tops of his boots and sewed them into a holster. He shaped a piece of wood to look like a Soviet revolver, which had a wooden grip, and stuffed it into the holster. "We will no longer beg for food," he declared. "We will demand it!"

Because he spoke Russian fluently, Selim would pretend to be a Soviet partisan and, with a veiled threat, order a farmer to hand over flour, peas, lard, salt, and other supplies. Seeing other "partisans" outside, the farmer would put the provisions on his horse-drawn cart, which the group took. When they reached the edge of the forest, they unloaded the cargo and sent the horse and cart back to the farmer. Although Selim acted gruff and menacing every time he confronted a farmer, he was always shaking from fear that someone would call his bluff.

As the nights grew longer and colder, Selim's mind often drifted back to the life he used to have three years earlier in the small Polish town of Raciaz. The freckle-faced, fair-haired boy lived with his parents and brother in a house in a lumberyard owned and operated by his father, Shmuel. Selim's mother, Hannah, was a warm, outgoing, well-read woman and one of the most respected people in town. At 14, Selim was looking forward to going to the same high school from which Musio had just graduated.

But then Germany invaded Poland. The simple, contented life that Selim and his family had known turned into a constant evasion of the enemy. Leaving behind their possessions, the Sznycers fled from town to town—Plonsk, Warsaw, Sieldce, Bialystok, and Rovno. Then it was on to Oszmiany, in the Soviet-occupied part of Poland, where they experienced some semblance of a normal life—that is, until Germany surprise-attacked the Soviet Union, and the family was once again uprooted.

Right after the Sznycers reached the town of Ilya, German troops marched in to a spirited welcome from non-Jewish Poles who gave the soldiers flowers and blew kisses. It was June 29, 1941—a bad way for Selim to celebrate his sixteenth birthday.

The Sznycers moved on, this time to the town of Kurzeniec where, despite the brutal treatment of Jews under Nazi rule, they found jobs. While their parents ran a government-owned shop that distributed bread to the Jews, Musio worked as a bookkeeper and Selim as a messenger boy, both at the town hall.

The brothers soon joined a secret group of Jewish youths who were in touch with several escaped Russian prisoners hiding in the surrounding villages. The young Jews planned to organize a partisan unit with the Russians the following spring to fight the Germans. They began stealing and buying weapons, which the brothers stored in the attic of the town hall because they had keys to the building. Selim and Musio told no one, not even their parents, about their plans.

One day while Selim was standing on the front steps of the town hall, several German officers pulled up in an open-air military vehicle. After showing them to the mayor's office, Selim went back outside. That's when he spotted it—a revolver just lying there in the open glove compartment. *Should I steal it? I'll never have a better chance. But if I do, the Germans will notice it's missing. If they suspect me, they'll kill me.* Despite his fear, he felt compelled to swipe it. His heart thumping wildly, Selim pulled out a rag and pretended to clean the vehicle. Making sure no one was looking, he placed the rag over the gun, which he then tucked in his belt under his overcoat. With nerves on edge, he fought the urge to dash off. *Don't run! Act calm.* He finished wiping an imaginary spot off the vehicle before walking inside to the room where Musio worked.

"I just stole a revolver from the Germans who are meeting with the mayor right now," Selim whispered in Musio's ear. "It's under my coat. What should I do?"

"Give it to me quick. I'll hide it." Musio put it in a drawer and then told Selim to run an errand and not return until after the Germans left. At the first opportunity, Musio hid the revolver behind some books.

When the officers discovered the gun was missing, they erupted in fury and frisked several of the town's employees. Figuring it had been stolen by partisans, the Germans jumped in their vehicle and left. After the mayor went home, Musio retrieved the revolver and stored it with the other hidden arms in the attic.

During their time in Kurzeniec, the Sznycers kept hearing reports of *akzias*—roundups of Jews who were then systematically murdered—in surrounding villages. Feeling helpless and desperate, Selim slept with his clothes on and kept a kitchen knife by his side. *If I die, I'll take some Germans with me,* he vowed.

In the spring, twenty young Jews, including Selim and Musio, began gathering nonperishable food and other supplies for their resistance group. The hardest part for them was not sharing their plans with their parents.

But the secret leaked out at home. Their father, Shmuel, was against it. "You have no right to break up the family," he stressed. "If we must die, we should all die together."

Musio protested, fueling an argument that grew so intense that Shmuel slapped him for the first and only time of his life.

Their mother, Hannah, though, sided with her sons. "Don't stay behind on account of us," she told them. "Our lives are almost over anyway. You're young. You should try to survive and fight and take revenge for all the Jews who've been senselessly killed."

"We will," Selim promised, adding that he wanted to save his parents. "Once we organize our unit and build our bunkers, we'll return for you."

When the Jewish leaders in Kurzeniec found out about

the plans, they forbade the young men from leaving, claiming, "If the Nazis know what you've done, they'll kill all your families." Selim, Musio, and the other members, fearing they could cause their parents' deaths, put their plans on hold.

Before dawn on September 9, 1942—the day before Yom Kippur, the holiest day of the year in the Jewish religion— Selim was awakened by a tapping on the window. His neighbor Doba warned that an *akzia* was under way. Selim's father, who had left at 4 A.M. to pray at the synagogue, was among the first held by the Germans who were now going door to door, rounding up Jews. There was no time to waste. Selim, Musio, and their mother fled into the wheat fields, hoping to reach the nearby forest. But when they came to a large open area, Hannah balked because it was heavily patrolled by soldiers. Hugging Selim and Musio, she said, "Go, my beloved children. Try to save yourselves and take vengeance for us. I won't survive anyway."

Despite her misgivings, they coaxed her to run with them. Crouching below the stalks in the fog, which muted the first light of dawn, the three took off. As they neared the other side, Selim glanced back and saw tears streaming down his mother's cheeks. She flashed a smile of encouragement, but her eyes were saying good-bye. Just then shots rang out. "They've seen us!" All three dropped to the ground and headed away from the gunfire. As bullets zinged overhead,

Selim low-crawled to a nearby barn and found Musio. "Where's Mother?" Selim asked.

Musio shook his head. "I don't know." Hearing a patrol just yards away, he whispered, "We can't stay here."

"But what about Mother?" said Selim. "How can we leave her all alone? She might need our help."

"We don't know where she is. If we go back, we'll be captured or killed. Remember what she said, 'Try to save yourselves.'"

More gunfire triggered Selim's instinct for survival. With Musio following, he scurried into a field on the outskirts of town and came to a seven-foot-tall fence. After Selim climbed over it, he heard "Halt!" In the lifting fog, he saw two German soldiers 30 feet away, lying on their stomachs behind a machine gun. The burst from their weapon nearly deafened him as he flattened himself on the ground.

Crawling along the bottom of the fence, he thought, *I have to go back over the fence before the morning gets any lighter or I'll have no chance.* He leaped to his feet and, amid a blaze of machine-gun fire, scaled the fence and flopped over to the other side, where Musio was waiting. Miraculously, Selim avoided getting hit.

The brothers dashed from barn to barn until they found one that was unlocked. Once inside, they burrowed in a 15-foot-tall stack of hay bales. In the distance, Selim heard footsteps, shots, and screams . . . people begging for their lives, soldiers laughing, guns firing . . . and then silence. That night he began smelling a horrible odor. *It's the smell of burning flesh! The Nazis are burning all the people they killed! Are Mother and Father among the dead?*

Through the day and night and all the next day, the brothers remained hidden in silent horror. *Those Nazis are so evil, they timed the massacre to occur right before Yom Kippur,* Selim thought. At midnight, the two left the barn and ran into the woods and slept under a tree. The next day they begged for bread and water from a peasant.

The brothers soon encountered a man from Kurzeniec who had hidden in the mayor's office during the *akzia*. He said all the Jews in town were herded into the market square. After young women and craftsmen were taken to a labor camp, the rest were put on trucks and driven to the outskirts of town where they were shoved into barns and gunned down inside. The bodies were then burned. "I overheard an officer boast that one thousand forty Jews were killed," he said.

Days later in the forest, another man who had witnessed the *akzia* broke the news that the brothers didn't want to hear but already knew in their hearts—their parents were among the slain. "They went to their deaths together," the man said.

"To us, they will always be alive," Selim told Musio before bursting into tears.

Musio held him and murmured, "We now have nothing left in our lives. Our main mission is to follow Mother's last request to save ourselves and take revenge on the murderers."

Eventually the brothers stumbled onto a campsite of Jews who had escaped. After building their own shelter out of branches, Selim and Musio begged for food from nearby farmers. It was getting colder by the day. Selim wore a thin coat, but Musio didn't have one. At night they slept on the ground by the fire, which they kept going until daybreak to stay warm and to ward off the wolves that roamed the area.

To most in the group, the situation seemed hopeless. They had no weapons to defend themselves, no shelter to stay warm in the coming winter, no money to buy food, and no way to stop the enemy—trigger-happy soldiers, anti-Semitic peasants, and "Jew hunters"—from tracking them down.

But the brothers refused to give up. They were determined to become full-fledged partisans in the spring—if they could survive the deadly winter. Selim and Musio decided to build a *zemlianka* with three comrades—16-year-old Zelig; his 30-year-old uncle Jeijze, who was a merchant; and Shimon, a 20-year-old blacksmith. It took them five days to hike to a forest near a swamp, where they constructed their underground shelter. Then, through stealing and bullying, they stocked it with enough basic provisions to last through the winter.

By mid-November Selim and Musio thought the group

had everything they needed, but the others insisted on getting just a few additional items, especially matches. So all five headed out in a snowstorm for one more trip. After obtaining two boxes of matches from a farmer, Selim put them in the pocket of his jacket and led the way back along a tree-lined road.

Suddenly, around midnight, they heard, "Kill them! Kill the Jews!" Out from behind the trees charged nearly two dozen peasants wielding sticks and sickles. Selim and the others bolted in different directions, each one chased by several peasants. Five relentlessly tailed Selim for one mile, then another. No matter how hard he ran, he couldn't lose them. In desperation, he threw off his jacket so he could go faster, but it did no good. Stumbling and tripping, he finally collapsed from exhaustion. When his pursuers caught up to him, they pummeled him with their sticks until he lost consciousness.

When Selim woke up, he was a bloody mess sprawled on his back in the snow. He had been stripped of all his clothes except his underpants. As his assailants discussed killing him, he thought, *I haven't done anything with my life. I didn't get to fulfill my promise to Mother. I didn't even get to kill a single Nazi.*

One of the attackers—a teenager like Selim—straddled him and then raised a knife to stab him in the chest. With death seemingly seconds away, Selim blurted out, "I want to live! I want to live! I want to live!"

His plea froze everyone. The young attacker, who was

still holding the knife high above him, got off Selim and said, "If you stop shouting, I won't kill you." Turning to his fellow assailants, he asked, "Now what do we do with him?"

"Bring him to the Germans and let them kill him," suggested one of the peasants. "If he's a Jew, they'll give us a reward—a bottle of vodka and some salt."

*That's all the life of a Jew is worth to these people?* Selim thought as two of them yanked him up and began dragging him in the snow. Energized by the cold and wind, he jerked free from their grasp and began running. Not hindered by heavy boots and clothes, he easily outdistanced them until they gave up the chase. He eventually made it back to the secret *zemlianka,* as did his comrades, who were also bruised and battered. Shimon suffered the worst. He was beaten and stabbed twice in the back and was also stripped of his coat. Selim, too, was without a jacket, which he had tossed away during the pursuit. With it went the matches.

For the next five months, the five lived in their crude shelter. They used metal buckets for cooking and fetching water from a nearby stream. They ate twice a day, usually potatoes and peas with a piece of meat or pork fat. Right after the evening meal, they would extinguish their lone kerosene lantern and chat in the dark before going to sleep. Once a week they boiled water to wash themselves and their clothes. A ditch several yards away acted as their bathroom. In the snow, they covered up their tracks by sweeping them with branches.

They wore only long underwear while they were inside, because it was less bulky than regular clothes and had less space for lice to hide. Every day they turned their underwear inside out and hunted for lice in all the seams and folds. Holding the underwear as close to the flames as possible, they roasted the lice, but within hours more lice were once again crawling on their skin.

Before going to sleep during those long winter nights, the young men talked about their lives and their families before the war. They also shared their dreams.

Jeijze and Zelig hoped to own a shop and become successful merchants.

"I wish for a breakfast of twenty scrambled eggs with sausage and butter and freshly baked bread," said Shimon. "Every day."

Musio imagined "living in Palestine as equal members of society in our own Jewish state."

"Me too," said Selim. "And I also dream of sleeping in a clean bed again, free of lice. They're nasty little creatures that drive people crazy and deserve to die."

"Like Nazis!" Musio cracked.

By mid-April the snow began to melt, signaling they had survived the harsh winter. After months of hibernating underground in total isolation, they left their *zemlianka* for good and tried to hook up with a partisan unit. But it wasn't easy. The leader of every group they came across said the same thing: "We don't accept anyone who doesn't have his own weapon."

Eventually, the brothers' three comrades left, so Selim and Musio teamed up with ten Jews who had escaped from a labor camp and were looking to join the partisans. In June, they met Commander Podolny, the leader of a partisan unit, who insisted they go on a trial mission first. "If you succeed, we will accept you in our unit," Podolny told them.

For their assignment, they had to sneak into the German garrison in Kurzeniec and burn the factory that produced wooden rifle butts. In addition, they had to cut down several telephone poles. The only weapons the young Jews were given were a revolver with one bullet and two hand grenades to use against a force of 200 soldiers and 50 policemen.

Selim dreaded returning to the town where he had spent the worst days of his life during the liquidation. But he and Musio wanted to prove they belonged as partisans. On the first night of their mission, German searchlights and flares lit up the sky near the factory, so the young men retreated and debated over a new plan.

"It's suicidal," claimed one. "Worse, we're likely to be captured alive."

"Yes," said another. "We don't even have enough ammo to kill ourselves."

A third added, "Even if we could torch the factory, the Germans will surround us before we can flee."

"We can't back out," Selim insisted. "This is our chance to show the partisans what we can do."

They worked out a compromise. Musio and six others left to cut down the telephone poles while the remaining five— including Selim and the group's leader, a young electrician named Yacub—sneaked over to the factory without being detected. Shimon Zimmerman, who was armed with a stick shaped like a rifle, stood guard in the yard. Carrying rags, cans of kerosene, and matches, the other four quietly pried open a window and climbed in.

But a shout from the night watchman broke the silence: "Bandits! Bandits!"

Petrified that they would be caught within minutes— after all, they were right in the middle of a German garrison—Selim thought about running away. Instead, he followed Yacub, who sprinted toward the watchman. During a surprisingly tough scuffle, Selim struck the man on the head with a grenade. Yacub then put his revolver to the man's temple and said, "We aren't bandits. We're partisans. If you don't stop yelling, I'll kill you."

Neighbors peeked out their windows, asking what was wrong. Shimon yelled to them, "Stay inside. We are partisans. If you disobey, we'll shoot you." They closed their windows.

The watchman shut up as Selim and his comrades spread rags along the wooden walls and poured gasoline over them. Then they lit the rags, igniting a blaze that spread with incredible speed. They let the watchman go. As the five fled the factory, they faced machine-gun fire, but they all managed to meet up with their seven comrades, who had sawed down a half dozen telephone poles, cutting off communication with the next town.

The young men hid in the woods for the rest of the day. The following night Shimon led them to the home of a friendly peasant who had news from Kurzeniec. "The word is that one hundred partisans attacked the town, and the Germans stayed in their bunkers to fight the large force."

"Yeah, all five of us." Selim chuckled.

The peasant continued, "The factory burned down, and the fire spread to other buildings because nobody dared leave their houses or posts to put it out. The night watchman survived and said he was attacked by dozens of partisans. Nobody could understand why the partisans didn't just kill him."

Yacub laughed. "I was saving the only bullet in my revolver for myself in case I was about to get captured."

For Selim, the mission was a turning point in his life. For the first time in three years of just trying to survive, he had actually attacked the Germans. "This is just the beginning of my revenge," he told Musio.

The dozen young Jews triumphantly returned to the partisan camp, expecting praise and acceptance as full-fledged fighters. Yacub went to brief Podolny, but returned with a different officer and several armed partisans who took away the Jews' two grenades and the revolver. The officer then chewed them out. "You did not follow orders. You were supposed to burn down the factory only, not part of the town! It was reckless of you and counter revolutionary. Now people will turn against us. I should have you all shot. But because you did destroy the factory and cut the telephone lines, I will show some mercy. Now go on your way. I don't want to see your faces ever again!"

"But we didn't set fire to the homes, only the factory," Selim protested. "The fire spread because the Germans and the townspeople didn't come out to douse the flames."

"Don't argue with me!" The officer and the other partisans aimed their weapons at the Jews. "Get out of my sight before I change my mind and have you all executed!"

Bitterly disappointed and discouraged, Selim and his comrades left. A few days later, they joined a group of escaped Jews in a makeshift camp in the woods. A person who knew Podolny told them why the partisans had rejected them: "Podolny is a Russian Jew. He would have accepted you, but his top officer refused to have any Jews in his unit. The officer agreed to send you on what he thought was a suicide mission. He was certain none of you would dare attempt it, which would have proven his claim that Jews are cowards. When you returned, Podolny wasn't there, so the officer took it upon himself to send you away."

The young Jews soon encountered a 12-person partisan unit of well-armed ex-military Russians headed by a cheerful but sometimes sadistic man named Suvorov. He selected Selim, Musio, and Shimon to guide their unit on a mission to acquire weapons that area peasants had collected from dead and fleeing Soviet soldiers who had retreated from the Germans the previous year.

The trio led the partisans to various villages and farms, where several peasants gave up their hidden arms, but only after they were threatened. In one case, a farmer denied having any weapons but no one believed him, so Suvorov grabbed him by the ear and shot a bullet through his earlobe. When the stunned farmer recovered from the shock, Suvorov said sarcastically, "Oh, I'm sorry. Somehow I missed shooting you in the head. I'll do better with the next shot."

"No, no!" pleaded the farmer. "I'll tell you where the firearms are."

The peasant at another house refused to cave in to Suvorov's threats and fearlessly told him, "Go ahead and kill me. I have no weapons to give you."

Suvorov and another partisan led him outside and forced

him to dig his own grave while Selim made the man's wife and children watch from the window. With the peasant facing his grave, Suvorov fired a shot. The man toppled in the hole as his wife and children wailed in horror. Suvorov then ordered Selim, "Bring out the woman. It's her turn now."

The woman broke down and tearfully begged for her life. "Please don't kill me!" she pleaded to Selim. "I know where the weapons are hidden!" She led the partisans to a pile of hay where two rifles were hidden. When she returned to the house, she almost fainted. There, sitting at the table, was her husband, unharmed. From her vantage point at the window she hadn't seen that Suvorov had deliberately shot between the farmer's legs and pushed him into the grave to make her think her husband had been murdered.

When the mission was over, the partisans had accumulated a substantial number of weapons. In appreciation for Selim's services, Suvorov gave him an old World War I Russian rifle. Musio received a rifle with a sawed-off barrel.

The brothers soon joined a new *otriad*—the Russian term for a partisan unit—made up of only Jews. Among them, the 90 men and 60 women had just 20 rifles, several handguns, and a few machine guns. Their *otriad* was part of a partisan brigade under the command of Colonel Markov, a former Polish teacher.

Teaming up with other *otriad*s of mostly non-Jews, Selim

and his comrades attacked a German garrison and ambushed patrols. They cut communication lines by chopping down telephone poles, and blocked roads by cutting trees. They burned wooden bridges that the Germans used.

Despite their successes, the Jewish fighters encountered anti-Semitism from members of other *otriad*s, who often tried to forcibly take away their weapons. Colonel Markov made it clear to the Jews: "Don't ever give up your weapon. Kill or be killed, but never give up your arms to anybody—even another partisan."

After just two months, Markov dismantled the all-Jewish *otriad* under orders from his superiors. Selim and Musio were transferred to a new unit of 80 Jewish partisans and 70 non-Jewish Russians headed by an anti-Semitic commander named Volodka.

He ordered the Jewish fighters to hand over all their valuables, such as gold, watches, and money, so that he could buy more weapons for the *otriad*. Each Jew was searched and anything of value was taken. Although Selim and Musio had nothing worthwhile, they were humiliated and infuriated. But there was nothing they could do, because any form of resistance was punishable by death. The Jews never got the promised arms. All the confiscated valuables went to Volodka and his friends.

Selim realized that anti-Semitism for many partisans

was stronger than their hatred of the Germans. Here he was, fighting side by side with Russians against a common enemy—the German war machine that was trying to annihilate all Jews and destroy the Soviet Union—and yet they despised him solely because of his faith. He had to repeatedly remind himself, *I'm fighting as a Jew with these partisans, but not for them. Someday I hope to have my own country to fight for—and even die for.*

Within a few months, Selim and Musio joined a new Jewish partisan unit that, along with other *otriad*s, attacked a German garrison in the town of Svoboda. They burned all the bunkers, blew up the watchtowers, and destroyed all the soldiers' buildings so that the enemy couldn't come back and use them.

After a year of victorious assaults, Selim and Musio faced their most perilous dilemma when, after a nighttime battle, they and 120 fellow partisans were surrounded by enemy forces and had nowhere to hide. The partisans were weary, hungry, and depressed. They knew that at first light, the Nazi troops would attack them. Their only hope was an audacious scheme—they had to trick the enemy.

Among the partisans were a dozen European fighters who took German uniforms out of their backpacks, complete with ranks and medals, and put them on. They also had German weapons. They disguised themselves as German officers in command of a Vlasov unit—a group of Russian soldiers who switched sides and fought against the partisans. Many members of the real Vlasov units still wore their Russian army uniforms but without any Soviet insignias.

Selim and several other partisans wore similar Russian uniforms, so they played the role of guards of this fake Vlasov unit. The rest of the partisans, including Musio, pretended to be prisoners. At daybreak, they were marched by the fake guards and fake German officers along the main road to a village where a group of Nazi-supporting Lithuanian soldiers was stationed. Although Selim was exhausted and nervous, he strode ramrod straight like a good German soldier. The "prisoners" slouched their shoulders and dragged their feet, which, given their real physical conditions, didn't require much acting.

In the village, the "German officers" cursed the "prisoners" and ordered them to halt. Then the "officers" demanded that the peasants feed the "guards" who had fought so bravely defending the villagers from these murderous partisans. The peasants were also made to feed the "prisoners." Selim and his comrades devoured potatoes, bread, butter, and milk— the first decent meal they had consumed in days.

With their bellies full, the fake Vlasov unit and its fake captives marched back out on the main road. Once they were out of sight of the enemy, they ducked into the fields and hiked 60 miles to the safety of the Rudnitzkaya forest, where other *otriad*s had gathered.

Fatigued but happy, Selim put his arm around Musio and exclaimed, "We did it! We outwitted the enemy and slipped right out from under their noses!"

Over the next two months, Selim's *otriad* blew up trains and tracks to disrupt the flow of German soldiers and supplies to the eastern front where the advancing Soviet army was hammering the Nazis.

During one of those missions, Selim personally laid a mine on the tracks near a train station outside the village of Mosti. Later that morning, from the vantage point of a nearby hill, he saw a train leaving the station. As it gathered speed and approached the mine, Selim held his breath. Suddenly, he saw a pillar of flames shoot into the sky and the locomotive rise off the tracks. A few seconds later, he heard a thunderous boom so loud it shattered windows in the village. To his supreme satisfaction, the engine toppled on its side and careened down an embankment, dragging with it a string of 30 cars, each one full of German soldiers, who piled on top of one another.

To Selim, the twisted, smoking wreckage was a sight to behold—an affirmation that he was fulfilling his pledge to seek revenge against the enemy by causing havoc and destruction wherever he went. Adding to his success, another troop train coming to evacuate the wounded and bring reinforcements was also blown up by a second mine placed by the partisans.

With Nazi forces reeling, the partisans moved westward, deeper inside Poland and behind enemy lines. For weeks of nonstop action, Selim, Musio, and their comrades continued to destroy communication and transportation lines as well as create panic by attacking retreating soldiers.

By the end of August 1944, following their latest triumph, Selim was exhausted. Trekking in single file for hours with 13 fellow partisans, the weary teenager could no longer keep pace. *I'm so worn out. I wish I could quit.* A few others slowed down, too. Eventually the line stretched so long that he lost sight of those in the front. A Russian partisan who always carried a guitar strapped to his back removed it and slung his carbine over his shoulder. Then he began to strum and sing Russian songs. Everyone joined in singing one of Selim's favorites: *"When Hitler will no longer be in existence, and in glorious victory we will return home, I shall remember my unit, and you my friend . . ."*

The more he sang, the more Selim picked up the pace. Soon everyone was marching in time in a line that was now tightened up. Selim no longer felt tired. He felt proud to be a partisan.

===

When the Soviets gained control of eastern Poland, the partisan otriads were disbanded. Selim and his brother, Musio, were drafted into the Second Infantry Battalion of the newly formed Polish army in September 1944. Promoted to corporal and then sergeant, Selim fought on the front lines in Germany until the end of the war.

Unable to legally leave communist-held Poland, Selim made contact with the Jewish Aliyah Organization, a group that smuggled Holocaust survivors out of Europe and into Palestine (which later became Israel).

Carrying fake papers and pretending to be, at various times, a Greek refugee, a former Hungarian prisoner, and a British soldier, Selim made his way to Palestine, fulfilling his dream of living in the Jewish homeland. He changed his name to Shalom Yoran. After Israel became a country in 1948, he joined the air force and learned aircraft maintenance and engineering. He met his wife, Varda, who was also serving in the air force, and together they raised two daughters. He then worked for Israel Aerospace Industries for more than two decades, becoming senior vice president and managing director of the maintenance and overhaul division.

In 1979 Shalom and his family immigrated to New York. Today, he and Varda, who is a noted sculptress and *artist, live in Brooklyn. His brother, Musio, who took the name Maurice Sznycer, is a world-renowned professor at the Sorbonne in Paris.*

*"I came to understand that if more Jews had defied extermination by resisting, many might have survived," Shalom once wrote. "If there is a lesson to be gleaned, it is that no person should succumb to brutality without putting up a resistance. Individually it can save one's life; en masse [all together] it can change the course of history."*

You can learn more about Shalom Yoran's life as a partisan in his book, *The Defiant* (Square One Publishers).

## "I CAN'T BECOME THE BEAST
## THAT I HATE SO MUCH"
# ROMI COHN

THE BURST OF GUNFIRE froze Romi Cohn for just a moment. It was enough time to see bullets riddle the three fellow partisans in front of him . . . enough to feel the burning impact of a round ripping into his knee . . . enough to realize *ambush!*

In a forest of Czechoslovakia's Tatra Mountains, Romi and his three comrades were on a patrol when they were assaulted by German commandos who had been lying in wait. Within seconds of the first volley, Romi sprang behind a tree. *I'll die if I stay and return fire,* he thought.

And so, despite the throbbing pain in his knee, he ran for his life deeper into the woods. Bullets whizzed by, snapping off snow-covered branches above him, splintering tree bark next to him, and ricocheting off boulders beside him. His heavy breathing nearly drowning out the gunfire, the terrified 15-year-old darted this way and that through the forest. But he couldn't shake the commandos who were determined to kill him. *They're gaining on me!*

Romi had chosen to put himself in harm's way. Although he knew the dangers and hardships that awaited him, he had joined the partisans because it was safer than the life he had been living in Pressburg, Czechoslovakia, where the Gestapo had been closing in on him. To Romi, it was better to fight and die than to live in terror of being hunted down in the streets of his hometown.

And yet, here he was being hunted down, this time in the woods. *Only God can save me now.*

It had been more than two years—a lifetime to a kid on the run—since he said good-bye to his four sisters; two brothers; mother, Emilia; and father, Leopold, a successful international businessman. Ever since the Germans took control of the country in 1939 when he was ten, life for Jewish families was a torment—from which the Cohns planned to escape.

In 1942 a guide was paid to help Romi, then 13, sneak across the border so he could live with relatives in Hungary, where it was safer for Jews. Once he made it, the rest of the family was supposed to follow.

Because the guide wouldn't permit any luggage, Romi dressed in three undershirts, three underpants, three shirts, two pairs of pants, and his best suit. Before he left, his mother took him aside out of earshot of the rest, hugged him, and whispered, "I have no hope left for the survival of our family or for any other Jews left in the city. We know what our destiny is. We are all doomed to be killed." Referring to the Jewish prayer recited for the dead, she told Romi, "At least one of us should survive to say Kaddish for the rest."

He would never see her or four of his siblings again. From that day on, Romi hid out in the homes of relatives and friends in one town or village after another. By luck and cunning, he always dodged German raids, many of which claimed the lives of those who had harbored him.

In the fall of 1944, he ended up alone back in Pressburg, pretending to be someone he wasn't. Supported by loans from a friendly banker, Romi rented a room and carried fake identity papers of a gentile (a non-Jew). He cut his hair and donned the clothes and hat that most of the non-Jewish teenagers wore in the city. He knew that one slipup, no matter how slight, could trigger suspicion and blow his cover.

In public, he never spoke to another Jew. If he saw someone he knew, he would walk by without acknowledging him. The only way he would talk to a fellow Jew was in a hidden alley or behind closed doors—and only after he was convinced that no one was following him. His rule of thumb: Trust no one.

One day while strolling down the street, he spotted Mr. Meir, a family friend who, like Romi, was disguised as a gentile. After making sure the Gestapo wasn't using Mr. Meir as bait, Romi went up to him and whispered, "Follow me." In the shadows of a nearby alley, they joyously embraced, each heartened that the other had survived, at least so far.

"Your family, is everyone safe?" Mr. Meir asked.

Romi cast his eyes downward, shook his head, and replied, "My father was captured by the police while he was trying to cross the border. The last I heard he was being held in a prison in Hungary." His voice cracked when he said, "I was told that my mother, my brothers, David and Yaakov, and my sisters Deborah and Hindi were taken to the Birkenau concentration camp and murdered." Managing a faint smile, he added, "My other sisters, Hanna and Sara, are hiding in Hungary. And what of your family?"

"We all live in the home of a gentile. But the landlord stole all our money, gold, silver, and jewelry. He said if we don't pay him the weekly rent, he'll kick us out. Romi, if that happens, we'll be picked up by the Gestapo in no time and carted off to the death camps."

"That's not going to happen." Romi reached into his pocket and pulled out all the money he had. "Here, take it."

"Oh, Romi, thank you, thank you!" As he counted the money, Mr. Meir's smile faded. "This will buy us only one week. I have to find a way to get more money for food or else my family and I are doomed."

"Don't worry. I'll get you the money."

As tears welled up in his eyes, Mr. Meir asked, "But how? Where?"

"I have my ways."

At the next meeting, Mr. Meir brought a friend, Yosef, who was in the same predicament as him—they needed money for food and rent. So Romi gave him cash, too. The relief and gratitude expressed by both men were tempered when they told him that other families they knew shared a similar plight.

*How can I get my hands on that much money?* he wondered. *And even if I can, how can I get it to those people without being discovered by the Nazis? I have to find a way.*

"I'll help them," Romi declared with confidence, even though he didn't know how he would do it. Then fate stepped in. While walking down the street, he bumped into Helena, a Polish gentile. She was a maid for Shlomo Stern, who worked in the Czech underground trying to save Jews. Through Helena, Mr. Stern agreed to give Romi the money for the two families so they could survive while remaining hidden.

But those Jews knew of others, who in turn knew of others in need of food, rent, and other necessities. Within weeks, 58 hidden Jewish families were relying on Romi to survive. Fortunately, he was able to fund his entire network through Mr. Stern, who had access to a large amount of money.

Operating this network put the 15-year-old at great risk. To lessen the danger, he made each family representative follow strict rules. Every rendezvous took place at night in dark alleyways out of the view of any passersby. No one could talk to him on the street unless he spoke first. If the person didn't show up, the meeting would be postponed to the next night. Failure to arrive the second night indicated the Nazis had captured the entire family.

Romi never wrote any notes or lists about his network. He memorized all 58 names and the times and places of each meeting. He chose not to know where the Jewish families were hiding so that if he were caught and tortured, he couldn't reveal their whereabouts.

While trying to keep his families alive, Romi was recruited by a friend in the Czech underground to be a courier. Romi would pick up a package from a secret contact and deliver it to another. He never knew what he was carrying or who he was meeting. The contact would wear a feather in their hat or a blue kerchief in their breast pocket.

He managed to avoid authorities until one afternoon, when his guard was down, he was stopped by two Gestapo officers who demanded his papers. Acting as casually as he could, Romi obliged. One of the officers snatched the papers and stuffed them in his pocket without even looking at them.

*Oh-oh, I'm in trouble,* Romi thought.

The officers each grabbed an arm and whisked him away. "What do you want of me?" Romi asked in Slovak. "What have I done wrong?"

"Don't hide behind the Slovak language," hissed one of the officers. "Speak to us in German, you cursed Jew."

*How could they know I'm a Jew? Was I given up by an informer or by someone in one of the families who was captured and tortured?*

As they hustled him off, Romi tried to stay calm and plot his escape. *I'll walk with them without any resistance so they'll relax their grip. Then I'll wait for the right moment to make a run for it. I can't make a mistake. I'll get only one chance.*

When they turned the corner, Romi's heart sank. They were heading toward Gehinnom, the Gestapo station where Jews were tortured. *No Jew comes out of there alive. I must escape. Anything less means certain death . . . and even worse. They'll torture me first. What secrets and information will they squeeze out of me that could lead to the deaths of my families? It doesn't matter. I need to act now! I'd rather get shot right here in the street than be tortured in Gehinnom.*

As they approached a throng of workers and shoppers, Romi took a deep breath and made his move. He yanked free from the officers' grasp and sprinted into the crowd. "Halt!

Halt!" shouted the officers. They began shooting at him as screaming people scattered or hit the ground. None of the people chased him, but the Gestapo officers did. They fired at least a dozen rounds, which all missed.

Romi, who knew the alleys in the city, ducked into a passageway that led to a maze of lanes and walkways. Turning left, right, left, he raced down the alleys until he lost his pursuers. When he came to a busy sidewalk, he melded into the crowd and strolled among the people so he wouldn't draw attention.

Though he had barely escaped with his life, Romi was in a terrible predicament. *I don't have any identification papers, so if I'm stopped again, I can't fake I'm a gentile. The Gestapo knows my false name, and they have my picture. I need a new name, identity, and a place to live. I can't go back to my room because they probably know my address. At least they won't find any notes about my hidden families.*

He couldn't return to collect his few worldly possessions. But with the help of the underground, Romi was given clothes and a new set of false ID papers. He dyed his hair and eyebrows red to create a different look.

Word eventually reached him that days before he was seized, the Gestapo had raided the home where one of his hidden families was staying. While being tortured, these Jews revealed they were receiving money from Romi. The

Gestapo then made his capture a high priority, plastering his photo on the walls in the city's police stations.

Every second of every day, Romi lived in fear that he would be captured, tortured, and murdered. He knew that any person he met could be his killer or betrayer—a Gestapo agent, a store owner, a landlord, or even another Jew. But still, he felt compelled to continue helping his hidden families.

Romi rented a new room in a small house, but told no one where he lived. It was on an upper floor with a window overlooking a backyard and was next to a drainpipe—perfect for a quick escape. He remained ever vigilant, even when he was sleeping, and trained himself to wake up at the slightest noise. He slept in his clothes and shoes, and kept his jacket and gloves by his bed.

Late one night, Romi was jarred awake by a loud banging coming from the front door on the first floor. *It's the Gestapo!* He put on his coat and gloves, climbed out the window, slid down the drainpipe, and silently scampered away.

The next day Romi wandered through the city with a dread feeling that the Gestapo was getting closer to catching him. *I must leave Pressburg. But what about my families? If I go, they won't get their money. And if that happens, they'll be tossed out in the street and captured. Hundreds of Jews will die. I need someone to take over for me. But who?*

Once again, fate stepped in. Romi bumped into Shlomo

Greenwald, a friend he hadn't seen in several years. Like Romi, Shlomo had false papers and dressed like a gentile. After hearing of Romi's situation, Shlomo agreed to take over the responsibility of delivering money to the hidden families.

Romi felt he could now leave Pressburg with a clear conscience. There was only one place left to go—to the mountains to join the partisans. Through a series of secret underground contacts, he traveled in the cold and snow to the remote home of a peasant named Nemchok, an ally of the partisans.

Soon two of the biggest men Romi had ever seen walked in. They were partisans whose hardened faces and angry eyes left no doubt in his mind that they would kill—and had killed—anyone in their way. "You're going with these men," Nemchok told Romi.

Moments later, Romi and the two partisans were on horseback heading silently along a mountain trail covered by more than a foot of snow whipped by a stiff wind.

Even though he was scared, he knew there was no going back, because there was nothing to go back to. No home, no family, no school, no friends. His anxiety about joining the partisans was eased by his belief that they would embrace him. *Surely the partisan leaders know of all the good work I've done in Pressburg. The leaders will be grateful and might even greet me with an honor guard.*

After hours on the trail, during which his companions never uttered a single word to him, one of them said, "We're here." Romi looked around and saw nothing but snow-covered trees. "Come," said the partisan. "We're taking you to central command." The other partisan brushed aside the snow, revealing a concealed door on a hillside directly behind a cluster of trees. It opened into a cave about 9 feet wide, 6 feet high, and 60 feet long lit by lanterns and two campfires. When they entered, Romi crouched low to breathe because smoke hung down from the cave's ceiling. He walked past a number of fierce-looking men who were cleaning their weapons. They paid him no attention.

Romi was ushered into the commander's room at the back of the cave. Behind a table made of rough unfinished wood sat Jan Husik, an imposing man in a military uniform. "Do you want to join us?" Husik asked in an unfriendly voice. When Romi nodded, Husik said, "What is your name?"

"Avrohom Cohn, but everyone calls me Romi."

"Give me your papers!" Husik barked. After scanning the documents, he thundered, "Liar! It says here your name is Jan Kovic." He slammed his fist on the table, causing papers and a mug to jump. "Your name is Jan Kovic! Do you understand? Now get out of here and get yourself a gun. Here you don't get food for nothing!"

At first, Romi was taken aback by the cold reception. He had assumed he'd be welcomed with a show of respect, maybe even made an officer for his anti-Nazi efforts in Pressburg. He certainly hadn't expected such rudeness. But upon reflection, he understood why. The commander didn't want anyone to know Romi was a Jew because there were anti-Semitic partisans in his ranks, and the unit couldn't afford to have any internal strife. As far as everyone was concerned, the new recruit was a teenage gentile named Jan Kovic.

In the main area of the cave, Romi approached the nearest partisan and asked, "Where do I get a gun?"

Everyone roared with laughter. *Why are they making fun of me? They're treating me like a child.* Again, he asked another partisan and another, but no one would respond with anything more than a laugh or a grunt. Finally he found someone with a friendly face and said, "My name is Jan Kovic, and I've just joined the partisans. The commander told me to get a gun, but whenever I ask how, everyone laughs at me."

The partisan squinted at Romi and said, "If you want a gun, you have to kill a German."

As Romi pondered exactly how he was going to kill a German without a weapon, he was taken to another cave. It sheltered ten partisans dressed in winter clothes and looking much like the men in the first bunker—coarse, brutish, and dangerous. They sat on the ground because there were no chairs, tables, or beds.

In response to a question from one of them, Romi puffed up his chest and said, "I was involved in the resistance in Pressburg and . . ."

To his shock, the men pounced on his bags and rifled through them, taking most everything he owned. Romi just stood there, stunned. *They're acting like savages, like hungry dogs tearing through garbage.*

Feeling a little sympathy for Romi, a lieutenant explained that these crude partisans were mostly local peasants who had little or no education and were accustomed to a relatively primitive lifestyle. Because Romi had come from the big city of Pressburg, they figured he had things of value in his bags. What they lacked in social graces they made up in ferocity. These men, mostly Slovaks and Czechs, were fighting for their homes and their land. Some were former Slovak army soldiers who had escaped when the Nazis conquered the country. The officers, however, tended to be educated and trained military men, many from Russia, who were sent to command the partisans.

"My men act this way because they are confined to this cave with nothing to do except clean their weapons for days at a time until they get an order to go out and fight," said the lieutenant. "They aren't allowed to leave to exercise or visit their families. If they did, the Nazis would discover our location. And if we have to fight the Germans on their terms, we will be annihilated. Many of my men have lost family members or comrades to the Nazi butchers. Partisans don't *have* to live this way. They choose to—so they can resist the Germans."

The lieutenant suggested Romi join his patrol unit, which went out every day to scout the mountains and valleys for German soldiers. "At least you won't be confined with the men in the cave. Most of the time you'll be outside on patrol."

"I want to join your group," said Romi.

"It's dangerous. You could freeze to death while asleep, get ambushed by the Germans, step on a mine, or get lost in the mountains. My patrol unit has by far the highest casualties of any partisan unit."

"I don't care," Romi declared. "I'm going with you. I'm not afraid. Besides, my only wish now is to kill the Nazis."

After collecting what few items the partisans hadn't taken from his bags, Romi walked out of the cave with the officer toward another bunker where the patrol unit lived. As the two tromped through deep snow, the officer said, "There are three rules that every partisan must follow. First, you must fight the Germans to your very last breath. Second, you must obey every order to the letter. Third, never, ever walk outside without a weapon. In fact, never let it out of your possession as long as you breathe. Anyone who violates any of those rules will be brought before a partisan military tribunal."

"And if the person is found guilty?"

"There is only one sentence—death by gunshot."

Later, inside the patrol's bunker, Romi met ten partisans who were much friendlier than those from the other caves. That night, Romi thought, *I'm not afraid of death. At least I won't die like a sheep led to slaughter. If I'm going to die, it will be with dignity as a man fighting against his enemies.*

The next day, armed with a Mauser semiautomatic submachine gun, he went out on patrol with two veteran partisans. Late in the afternoon, they cautiously entered an isolated village and were soon greeted warmly by the peasants who fed them and gave them food to take back to their comrades.

Before returning to camp, the trio headed out in the blowing snow and plunging temperatures to check out a report from the peasants that German soldiers were camped on the other side of the mountain. A few hours later, the patrol reached a ridge, but the storm and darkness made it impossible to see the Germans. The three partisans spent the night curled up under the thick branches of pine trees. Although snow had slid into Romi's boots and melted, he didn't care. He was so exhausted that he quickly fell asleep.

Shortly before daybreak, he was shaken awake. When he stood up, he discovered that the snow in his boots had frozen his socks, causing his feet to hurt with every step. There was nothing he could do but tolerate the pain.

At dawn, the trio peeked over the ridge and spotted 12 German soldiers in the campsite below—too many to attack. The patrol headed back. For hours and hours the men slogged through the deep snow, their weapons and bags of food feeling heavier with each mile. The pain in Romi's feet intensified until it became so unbearable that he collapsed. "I can't take another step," he moaned. His comrades looked at him with disdain. "We're not waiting for you to feel better," snapped the patrol leader. "If we leave you, the Germans will capture you and torture you until you tell them everything you know." He ordered the other partisan, "If he can't keep up, shoot him."

The partisan took the safety lock off his weapon and asked Romi, "Can you walk?"

Romi knew if he answered no, he would be executed. So he willed himself to rise and, despite the excruciating pain, marched on until they finally reached their bunker. Once inside, he was too weak to remove his boots and socks because they were still frozen to his feet. He sat next to the fire for 20 minutes until the ice melted enough for his comrades to pull off his boots. Now he could see why he was in such agony—he was suffering from frostbite and bleeding wounds on both feet. The commander ordered him to stay in the bunker for a day to recover while a larger number of partisans went out to attack the German campsite.

The mission was a success, although costly. All 12 enemy soldiers were killed, while the partisans lost two men and had two more wounded. The unit brought back all the Germans' possessions—guns, ammunition, hand grenades, tents, and food. Romi was surprised that none of the partisans talked about their two dead comrades. Instead, as they sat in their smoky bunker, they relived the battle and boasted about the supplies they had gathered.

"The Waffen-SS will retaliate for those killings," said an officer, referring to an elite Nazi force. "It'll probably be against the villagers who told us about the German soldiers. The SS will take some hostages—old men, young girls, it won't matter—and kill them as an example to everyone in the area who would dare talk to us. It's not about punishment. It's about terror."

With every passing day, Romi felt a growing acceptance by members of the patrol unit, even though he was by far the youngest. One day they presented him with a horse—an important status symbol among the partisans. Delighted and proud that they thought enough of him to give him a horse, he jumped onto the animal's back. Neighing and snorting, it reared up and bucked, throwing Romi to the ground. His comrades roared with laughter and admitted to him that this horse was so stubborn and mean that no one could ride it for more than a few seconds.

Ignoring the bruises on his body and to his ego, Romi tied the horse to a tree and vowed to tame it. Every day for two weeks he petted it and gave it a piece of sugar until he gained its trust. Then he climbed on its back and took hold of the reins. His fellow partisans stopped what they were doing, expecting to see the horse throw him off again. But it obeyed Romi's every command. Earning newfound respect, Romi was now one of the few partisans who owned a horse.

Throughout the region, the partisans had become so effective in ambushing the enemy that the German soldiers feared them. The precision hit-and-run attacks disrupted German convoys and left scores dead.

Romi was an observant Jew, but he had no conflict about killing others. He believed that in times of peace, an observant Jew must serve his God, but in times of war, his religious duty was to fight the enemy to save his life and the lives of others.

Late one afternoon, Romi's patrol came across a large number of footprints in the snow leading to a mountain pass where more than 100 German soldiers were camping for the night. The patrol quickly returned to the command center to report its findings. It was decided to spring a trap. Under cover of darkness, the partisans ran ahead of the enemy camp and, in three-man teams spaced 15 yards apart, settled into positions behind trees and boulders on a hill overlooking the pass.

Early the next day, the German soldiers moved out toward the hidden partisans. As Romi lay covered in snow, he could feel his heart pounding. He had never faced this many enemy soldiers before. But he wasn't scared; he was excited. Here was a chance to exact revenge on a large scale.

"Fire!"

On that command, Romi leaped from his hiding place amid a roar of gunfire and quickly emptied the clip of his weapon. He ducked behind a boulder and reloaded. Along with his comrades, he once again fired at will while the confused and panic-stricken Germans below tried to flee in all directions.

Within ten minutes, about 100 Germans lay dead. Among the bodies, Romi heard the cries of wounded Germans begging for mercy. He was infuriated by their pathetic pleas. *These are the same men who laughed as they gunned down helpless men, women, and children.* He spat in the snow.

The wounded didn't stay wounded for long. Any fallen soldier who moved was shot by the nearest partisan. As

Romi walked through the carnage, he felt a sense of power and strength. The Nazis, who appeared so invincible when they were murdering Jews, now seemed so weak and helpless. *These Nazis showed just how cowardly they really are when confronted by those who fight back.* He spat again.

Carrying all the German gear and supplies they could manage, the partisans made a triumphant return to their bunkers. But they couldn't gloat for too long. They knew that the few soldiers who had escaped would alert the German command, which would order a vicious retaliation.

Soon the partisan lookouts reported that a convoy of 200 SS troops was moving into the mountains. These particular soldiers were known as cold-blooded killers who pursued their prey with suicidal fervor.

But the partisans weren't intimidated. In fact, they turned the SS troops' blind vengeance against them. Six snipers stationed at the edge of the forest fired on the convoy. The enemy soldiers leaped out of their trucks and chased after the fleeing snipers, who dashed into the woods, across a wide mountain meadow, and up a hill. As the enemy reached the bottom of the hill, Romi and his comrades waiting in ambush opened fire from above, sending the SS troops into chaos. When the Nazis tried to retreat, they were mowed down by partisan machine gunners who were hiding in the woods. Almost all the soldiers were killed, while the partisans lost only three men. The victors took two days to strip the battlefield of all the German equipment and supplies.

The Nazi command decided against sending such a large force into the forests. Instead, it deployed faster, smaller crack commando units to infiltrate the mountains and ambush the partisans.

On a winter afternoon in early 1945 Romi and three others on patrol stumbled into one of those deadly traps. His comrades were killed instantly, and he was shot in the knee. Although he was always told never to retreat toward the partisans' camp, Romi, in his frightened, unthinking state, did just that. The commandos remained in hot pursuit, firing at him as he zigzagged through the forest despite the sharp pain in his leg. Only after he raced across a meadow and into more woods did the commandos stop on their side, knowing he'd have a clear shot at them.

After making it back to the bunker, Romi was treated by the medic, a partisan who had taken a course in first aid. As the medic cleaned Romi's wound with vodka, he discovered that the bullet had penetrated the flesh and missed the bone by a single millimeter.

While Romi was recovering, one of the partisans, a German-born communist who made it clear he hated Jews, became uncharacteristically friendly, constantly asking questions about the young man's family and background. If there was one skill that Romi had acquired over the years, it was his ability to detect danger.

*It's not a question of* if *he will try to kill me, but* when, thought Romi. *I must find a way to protect myself.* Romi remembered the ammo clip with the rusted bullets he had found on patrol a few weeks earlier. Even though rusted bullets tended to explode if fired, he had kept them in the bottom of his backpack. *They're the answer!*

While everyone was asleep, Romi crawled toward the German partisan's rifle and secretly placed three of those rusted bullets in its chamber. The next day during target practice, the chamber of the German's rifle exploded, badly injuring the partisan's face and putting him out of commission. He was no longer a threat to Romi.

A week later, having recovered from his own bullet wound, Romi was on patrol with fellow comrade Franti Cek when they captured two German soldiers. Romi tied the soldiers' hands behind their backs and blindfolded them before he and Franti brought them to the partisans' commander, Captain Cherpansky. When he was through grilling them, Cherpansky ordered Romi and Franti to take one of the prisoners, who was bound and hooded, away. Turning to Romi, the commander said, "I am giving you the honor of executing him."

Franti grabbed the German by the arm and led him into

the forest. "This is a great honor to give such a young recruit," Franti told Romi. After Franti secured the prisoner to a tree, he pulled the cover off him. The German's eyes were wide in stark terror. "Please don't kill me!" he begged. Tears streamed down his cheeks.

*How many times did this German see that look in the eyes of defenseless women and children?* Romi wondered. *Did he ever show compassion toward them?*

The entire company of partisans had gathered to witness the execution. They believed that the Nazis were cruel beasts who didn't deserve the dignity of a fatal bullet. No, this Nazi would die by having his belly slashed open by a partisan.

Facing the whimpering prisoner, Romi thought about his murdered mother and siblings, and of the times his father was heartlessly assaulted by police. He recalled that awful day when he was nine and members of the Hlinka Guard—thugs, really—burst into his school and beat up the children. *Innocent children!* And he thought about all his relatives whom the Nazis had tortured and killed.

Romi reached into his boot and pulled out his knife. Yes, he could get some small measure of revenge by executing this squirming German soldier. But suddenly Romi came to a profound realization: *I can never kill this way. I cannot lower myself to slaughter this pathetic excuse for a human being, no matter how much he deserves it. I can't become the beast that I hate so much.*

He turned and handed his knife to Franti and said, "You can have the honor." As Romi walked away, he heard an agonizing scream.

It was on a brisk spring day in 1945 when Romi was given the big news. The partisan in charge of the radio burst out of the command bunker, shouting, "The war is over!"

For Romi, it took a few minutes for those four words to sink in. *The . . . war . . . is . . . over.* For six horrific years, his childhood was defined by unending fear, brutality, terror, and sorrow. Now, this real-life nightmare was over. Or was it? The war might have ended, but he knew the heartache over the loss of loved ones would hurt forever.

The partisans were jubilant. Enduring the most difficult conditions possible, they had helped defeat the Nazis. But they paid dearly for the victory. Commander Cherpansky's force had numbered 250 partisans when it was formed. By the war's end, only 32 had survived, including late recruits like Romi. Every partisan had suffered at least one serious wound. Of the unit's 30 horses, only 2 survived—1 of them Romi's.

As the partisans proudly headed out of the mountains, they were welcomed in every village and treated like national heroes. Romi considered himself a victorious liberator. Despite the harsh conditions and the dangers of battle, his months with the partisans were, in some ways, the best of his young life. His blood coursed with pride and glory, and his soul was warmed by a destiny fulfilled. *I fought back against those who sought to destroy me and my people. I helped defeat the enemy of God.*

≡

*After the war, Romi, who was honored with several medals for bravery, was reunited with his father and two of his sisters in Pressburg (now known as Bratislava, Slovakia).*

*His oldest sister, Hanna, had escaped to Budapest, Hungary, where she lived as a Catholic with a gentile name. In 1944 an informer turned her in and Hanna was sentenced to death. But her friends bribed officials into releasing her. She hid in Romania until the war ended.*

*Sara, his second-youngest sister, had been smuggled into Hungary by the Cohn family's former housekeeper, a gentile who raised Sara as her own throughout the war.*

*His father had been arrested in Budapest without any charges other than being Jewish. He suffered daily rounds of psychological and physical torture before he was transferred to a work camp, where he toiled under inhumane conditions. It took him months after the war to recover.*

At age 16, Romi started his own business to support the surviving members of his family. He began buying and selling hard-to-find items such as soap, cigarettes, and matches on the black market. In no time, he had built up a remarkably successful business. When his father recovered, they owned and operated a thriving company that manufactured fur goods.

Although they were wealthy, Romi and his family were not happy living in Pressburg. They could never be at peace in that city because there were too many bad memories, so they eventually immigrated to New York. After graduating college, Sara moved to Israel, where she became a still-life artist. Hanna married and raised a family. Romi's father remarried and had six children by his second wife. He died at age 96.

After marrying his Belgian-born wife, Mavina, Romi founded and ran a highly successful home-construction business. They both became American citizens. A deeply religious man, Romi is a rabbi who often speaks to groups about his experiences during the war. "More than simply remember the Holocaust," he says, "we must remember the lessons of the Holocaust."

You can read a more in-depth account of Romi Cohn's life as a partisan in his book, *The Youngest Partisan* (Mesorah Publications).

# "IF I DIE NOW, I'LL FALL AS A FIGHTER"
# SARAH (SONIA) SHAINWALD

DAY AFTER DAY AS the battle raged, teenage partisan Sonia Shainwald did all she could to ease the suffering of her wounded comrades. And yet, she felt so helpless.

Her tattered uniform soaked with the blood of the fallen, Sonia worked tirelessly alongside an overburdened doctor in a bleak and busy field clinic. Ignoring the enemy mortar shells that exploded nearby, she bandaged blown-off limbs, dressed gaping wounds, and assisted the doctor in extracting bullets buried in flesh.

With medicine and medical supplies scarce, she resorted to desperate measures. The moment a fighter died, Sonia unwrapped the bloody bandages, washed them, and used them on the next wounded partisan. Often, though, swiftness was so critical to saving a life that she didn't even have time to clean the bandages before putting them on a new patient.

In too many cases, the valiant efforts of the shorthanded

and under-equipped medical staff were in vain. Sonia knew it, and the wounded partisans knew it, too. For those who were beyond saving, she knelt beside them and held their hands, offering them comfort in the final moments of their lives.

The wagonloads of wounded kept coming and coming, dropping off 10, 20, 30 wounded at a time. *When will this end?* Sonia wondered. *When will this ever end?*

Sarah Shainwald grew up in Luboml, Poland, a close-knit rural town where everybody knew everybody. (It is now in Ukraine.) Of its 7,000 citizens, 4,000 were Jews, mostly craftsmen and merchants who resided near the marketplace and in the shadow of the Great Synagogue.

Sarah lived in a cocoon of love spun by her parents, Wolf and Beila, her two older brothers, Shneyer and Meir, her large extended family of 60 aunts, uncles, and cousins, and her Jewish friends in school. Wolf worked in the lumber business while Beila maintained a spotless two-bedroom house filled with fragrant plants and flowers. She felt joy serving her family delicious dinners on white linen.

Frail and skinny, Sarah often suffered from coughing fits, shortness of breath, fatigue, and high fevers. Because she was the youngest and most fragile, her parents pampered and spoiled her. Far from being jealous, her brothers were always kind to her. Surrounded by all this love, Sarah pictured herself living in Luboml the rest of her life.

But anti-Semitism began spreading in the region like a cancer. Punks attacked her brothers and other Jews. At a school assembly, her own principal told the students that all the Jews should leave and go to Palestine.

Despite the bigotry, Sarah enjoyed school because she loved learning. In the spring of 1939, when she was 14, she passed a series of difficult exams that led to her acceptance into the town's only academic high school. She couldn't wait for classes to begin in the fall, because she would be studying her favorite subjects—literature, history, geography, and science.

Sarah never got the chance to attend. Just days before high school was to start, the Germans invaded Poland from the west. Less than three weeks later, the Russians invaded from the east, splitting the country in two. For the next 21 months, Luboml was occupied by the Soviets, who drafted Shneyer into the Red Army.

In June 1941, the Shainwalds' world exploded when war broke out between the Germans and Russians. Within 72 hours, the Wehrmacht (Nazi Germany's armed forces) marched into bomb-ravaged Luboml, having vanquished the Russians there. Jewish refugees fleeing the town were strafed by the Luftwaffe (German air force) and beaten up by Nazi-sympathizing Ukrainian gangs.

Despite the danger, the Shainwalds left in a horse and buggy after burying their valuables under a shed next to their house. They were trying to reach the railroad station in the nearby town of Kovel, 30 miles away, to catch a Russia-bound train, but they arrived too late. The last train had left just minutes earlier.

Distraught that they had missed an opportunity to escape, the family headed back to Luboml only to face columns of German soldiers marching in the opposite direction. As the Shainwalds passed them, the soldiers struck them with rifles, clubs, and whips until all of them—mostly Wolf and Meir—were bloodied.

When the family returned home three days later, they were shocked. Much of the town, including the heart of the Jewish section, was burned to the ground. And so was their house. Only one stone step remained. Nothing else was left, not even their valuables. Sarah's childhood home—in fact, everything she had ever known as a child—was now in ruins.

It would only get worse. The Shainwalds were forced into a ghetto, where they lived with 12 other Jews in a small house of less than 700 square feet (the size of a typical classroom). Everyone was forced to work for the Nazis. Despite her fragile condition, Sarah lugged steel rails, pushed loaded wheelbarrows, and unloaded heavy equipment from trucks ten hours a day until she collapsed from a back injury that would trouble her the rest of her life.

Her brother Meir, who toiled all day at a sawmill with his father, was often beaten by guards until he was a shell of his former self. No longer was he the happy-go-lucky young man who made Sarah laugh. Now when he came home, he didn't speak or smile; he just flopped on the bed and faced the wall.

In the ghetto, everyone was underfed and undernourished. Because of the horrible conditions, Sarah was constantly sick with fever and respiratory infections and, like many people, suffered from depression.

Every day brought new terror. Groups of Jews regularly were rounded up by the hundreds and executed. On Wednesdays a sadistic Wehrmacht officer would come into the Jewish quarter and simply shoot people for sport. Reports began filtering to the Shainwalds that whole populations of Jews in surrounding towns had been murdered.

But nothing hurt the family more than when they received dreadful news: Shneyer had been captured by the Germans and sent to a POW camp known for its inhumane treatment of prisoners. Although there was no official confirmation, he likely was dead. His probable death sent Sarah spiraling into an emotional hole of despair and hopelessness.

In September 1942, Meir announced to Sarah and his

parents that he and 30 friends were escaping from the ghetto to fight with the partisans, even though the young men had only one weapon among them. Wolf and Beila supported his decision, believing it was his best chance at surviving.

"Take me with you," pleaded Sarah. "I'll do anything to get out of this doomed place."

As much as it pained him, Meir refused. "I wish I could, but I can't, Sarah," he said. "You're too young and too frail. Besides, the group agreed not to take any girls under eighteen. You'll be a liability. The partisans would never accept you. I'm sorry."

No amount of begging and crying by Beila and Sarah could convince him to change his mind, although he clearly was anguished. Sarah could see the torment in her brother's eyes. She knew he wished he could help his kid sister and his parents, but there was no way. Still, when he walked out the door, she felt bitter.

Days later, on the Jewish holiday of Hoshana Rabbah, the liquidation of Luboml's Jews began. Just before dawn, the Shainwalds heard dozens of trucks enter the town. "The SS and Ukrainian police are here to kill us all," Wolf warned. "It is time for us to hide."

He had built a special place under a pile of 15-foot-long wooden planks that abutted an unfinished addition to a house. Inside this cramped space, Sarah and 15 others sat silently on the earthen floor, their knees close to their chests in two rows facing one another. There was no food, no water. Figuring they would have to be concealed for several long hours, maybe an entire day, they remained mute while listening to the pandemonium outside of gunfire, shouts, and wails. It never let up. The "Jew hunt" went on through the night and into the next day and the day after.

By now thirst and hunger—especially thirst—had consumed everyone in the hiding place. Adding to their misery, the stench from human waste and sweat had made it almost unbearable to breathe without gagging. After nightfall of the second day, Sarah told her father, "The stench will give us away. They'll realize it's coming from humans and find us." Then, for the first time in her life, she gave advice to her father: "*Tateh*, we have to get out of here now, whatever the danger."

He agreed. About half the group stayed in the hiding place while the others slipped out. The Shainwalds crawled through a break in the ghetto fence and continued to creep several hundred yards to the last street. They needed to get past a Ukrainian policeman, who had orders to shoot to kill any escaping Jew.

Wolf approached him and, bribing him with a roll of phony American money, was allowed to cross the road alone with the assurance that Sarah and her mother could follow.

But when the two tried, the policeman pointed his rifle at them and ordered them to lie down in the gutter. Sarah looked up and recognized him as the same person who used to play soccer with Shneyer when they were youths.

"What will you gain by killing us?" Beila asked him. She begged for their lives and kissed his uniform, hands, and boots. Then she offered him her wedding ring, which he quickly pocketed. Firing his weapon deliberately over their heads to make it look like he was doing his job, he let them join Wolf on the other side of the road.

The trio ran across fields and pastures, but they were weak from not eating or drinking for the previous 48 hours. Their throats were parched, so when they came upon a pond filled with green slime, they didn't hesitate to drink from it. They eventually reached the home of Wolf's friend and ate their first decent meals in days.

Once they were fortified, they continued their 12-mile trek to a village where they reunited with Beila's brother Hershel, a former scout in the Polish army who had been hiding with gentile friends. Hershel, though, was a crushed man. He was filled with rage and guilt because he had been unable to save his beloved wife and two small children from being murdered by the Nazis just days earlier.

Unfortunately, there wasn't room for the Shainwalds to join him in his hiding place. Their only option was to live in the woods throughout the bitter winter. Most fugitives considered that a death sentence—a slow and agonizing one.

Although Hershel could have remained hidden with his friends, he chose not to stay because Sarah and her parents were all he had left to live for. So he went with them, hoping to use his survival skills and knowledge of the forest to keep them alive in the wilderness.

With no plan and little food, the four hiked deeper into the woods, picking berries and mushrooms along the way. A few days later, they encountered a kind Ukrainian peasant named Tichon, who lived with his wife, Fedora, and three children in an isolated cottage. He looked at the group with pity. "You older folks at least have had a chance to live, but why does that young girl have to suffer?" Tichon said. "What sin did she commit?"

He promised to watch over them and bring them food once they set up shelter deeper in the forest. He told them they could come regularly and help themselves to the potatoes he stored underground in the bin next to his home. But he cautioned that the local police visited him frequently to buy the illegal liquor he made. "I'll give you a signal," he told the four refugees. "If the broom by the front door is leaning against the wall with the handle up, it means the coast is clear. If the handle is down, stay away."

After finding a spot deeper in the woods, Hershel

constructed a low hut of branches, twigs, leaves, moss, and bark with a small pitched roof to shed the rainwater. It was so tiny that the four of them could sleep only on their sides together with their coats piled on top of them. If one person turned over, the others had to turn over, too.

Whenever unfriendly peasants, bounty hunters, or Nazi henchmen came near, the family had to move away quickly. About every two weeks, they built a new hut, which was always within three and a half miles of Tichon's home. Never knowing what would happen minute to minute, Sarah remained on edge and in constant fear of being caught.

As the brutal winter set in, Sarah worried they would die from the cold. At times, their flimsy hut was completely covered by windswept snowdrifts. To ward off temperatures that remained below zero for days at a time, Tichon brought them bundles of straw, which they used for insulation and to seal the hut's entrance. Fedora wove Sarah a pair of large straw slippers to keep her feet warm.

The foursome built fires to cook their food and warm their bodies only in the twilight hours, when it was hardest for the enemy to spot smoke or the flames' glow. But Sarah could never get warm, causing chronic pain in her fingers, back, face, and feet. Even when she sat close to the flames, she still felt numb. Once she singed her legs without realizing it, leaving burn marks on her skin for several years.

For meals, her uncle packed a small metal pot with potatoes, sealed it with leaves and moss, and turned it upside down over the campfire. Beila also made potato soup. Most Sundays Tichon and his wife brought them pierogi, Polish dumplings. As much as the family needed the protein, they would not eat pork, which is forbidden in the Jewish faith. Turning down any non-kosher meat was one of the few connections they still had to Judaism.

After sneaking into a nearby village one day, Hershel returned with yarn and knitting needles for Sarah and her mother to make sweaters, which he traded with peasants for bread and meat. If he was given pork, he passed it on to Tichon.

Sarah and her family spent the long, miserable winter sitting in the hut, seldom speaking, lost in their own thoughts, and fighting depression. They also stayed mum because they didn't want their voices to give them away.

Even though the harsh winter threatened their lives, there were times when nature's majesty and beauty awed Sarah. She marveled at the stark splendor of a sun-kissed morning following a heavy snowfall, the sparkling charm of icicles dangling from branches, the rich green pine trees contrasting with the snow-white landscape. She watched in fascination as squirrels burrowed in the hard ground to find long-buried nuts, birds built nests that protected their young, and foxes frolicked in the snow.

For entertainment, Sarah killed lice. No matter how often she scrubbed her undershirt with snow and hung it on a tree to dry, the insects and their eggs returned.

By early March 1943, the family had survived the worst of winter. Just when Sarah was beginning to feel slightly more confident, Tichon showed up and warned, "You have to leave because the area has become infested with Bulbutzye." He was referring to bands of bloodthirsty, Nazi-sympathizing Ukrainian nationalists on the prowl for Jewish refugees. "They just killed some Jews who had lit a fire at the wrong time. I heard they're hunting specifically for you."

The foursome moved on until they found shelter in the barn of a poverty-stricken widow with five children. To Sarah, living in a hayloft was heaven compared to their winter huts. Her father and uncle made nightly trips to other farmers, begging for grain or stealing it. Whatever they brought back was ground into flour and turned into bread, which they gave to the widow as "rent."

Later that spring, Tichon arranged for them to meet an officer of a Soviet partisan brigade that was in the area. Taken to a prearranged spot in a clearing, they waited for hours before an officer arrived on horseback. When he dismounted and saw four malnourished wretches with long, filthy hair, he wasn't impressed. "How many Germans have you killed?"

he asked. Their silence answered his question. He then said, "Let's see your weapons." Again he was met by silence.

*We'll definitely be rejected,* Sarah thought.

But then Hershel mentioned his experience as a scout in the Polish army and his vast knowledge of the region. The partisan nodded and told them to follow him. Walking over ground that had barely begun to thaw, they reached a bustling camp in the midst of Nazi-occupied Ukraine. Sarah was stunned to see dozens of people moving about freely, cooking, baking, and laundering. She walked past tailors, shoemakers, and nurses. The camp hummed with activity that she hadn't seen in two years. Most heartening for Sarah was seeing the rifles in the hands of young men dedicated to fighting the Germans. Armed resistance—only a fantasy to her before—was now a reality, and she was thrilled that she would finally contribute to the cause.

A partisan holding a notebook wrote down their names. When Sarah gave her name, the partisan shook his head. Because Sarah was a Jewish name, he declared, "Here, there are no Sarahs. You will be called Sonia."

Sarah couldn't object and wasn't sure she wanted to. She already felt like a changed person, and the new Russian name seemed to fit her new life. *I am now Sonia. I am now a partisan!* She liked the sound of that.

The battalion, which had about 100 members, was one

of 12 units of varying sizes in the Fyodorov-Chernigovsky brigade, with a combined force of nearly 1,800 Soviet soldiers and anti-Nazi Poles, Ukrainians, Belorussians, and Jews. Despite their different backgrounds, they mostly got along because the commanders didn't tolerate any ethnic or religious infighting. The battalion's role was to help cripple the German war effort by blowing up trains and disrupting the movement of soldiers and supplies.

Sonia and her family were assigned their own tent, which became a magnet for young partisans, especially the battalion's two dozen Jews. Many were sole survivors from large families murdered by Nazis.

One of the nightly visitors was Piotr Menaker, a slender Jew in his early twenties who, as a Red Army lieutenant, had escaped from a German POW camp and joined the partisans. A romantic at heart, he fell for Sonia. He recited poetry, much of which he penned himself, and serenaded her with ballads that he played on his guitar. An impressionable teenage girl who had just survived a winter in the woods, Sonia was smitten. However, neither could act on their growing affection for each other because Sonia's parents were always only a few feet away. There was never any hand-holding and certainly no kissing. Sonia's parents liked Piotr and told her they would approve of a marriage between the two, but only when she was older. Besides, there was a war to fight first.

The family did their part for the cause. Hershel went out on daily missions because he knew the land far better than anyone else in the unit. Wolf was a member of a group that raided surrounding farms for livestock and canned goods. Sonia and her mother worked as assistant medics and cooks. Few women in the battalion engaged in combat. Most worked as support staff, gathering and chopping wood, collecting water, washing clothes, and cooking meals.

Early on, Sonia went on a mission with a team to derail a train. She acted as a medic even though she had no medical training. Because she had no gun to defend herself, Sonia was issued two hand grenades—one for the enemy and one to blow herself up to avoid capture.

The team successfully completed its mission, but on their way back, the partisans were attacked by the Bulbutzye. Although this was her first combat experience, Sonia wasn't scared and barely lowered her head for cover. During the firefight, she thought, *If I die now, I'll fall as a fighter, not at the hands of some Nazi executioner who thinks Jews are unworthy to live.* Fortunately, the enemy was driven off and the partisans returned unharmed.

Whenever Hershel encountered the enemy, he was fearless in battle, earning the admiration of his comrades for his bravery. One day, about two weeks after joining the partisans, Sonia and her parents went out to greet Hershel and the fighters on their return from their latest mission. But Hershel wasn't with them.

The head of the battalion, Commander Popov, took the Shainwalds aside and explained that Hershel's unit had been ambushed by the Bulbutzye. Hershel was wounded but rather than seek cover as his comrades urged, he charged at a machine-gun nest and was fatally mowed down.

The news rocked Sonia's mother so much she collapsed. When she recovered, she began wailing until Popov ordered her to stop. "Your brother died a hero," the commander said. "We don't cry here. We just carry on." To the partisans, a display of sorrow was a sign of weakness and wasn't tolerated.

*Uncle Hershel had nothing more to live for,* thought Sonia. *After his family was murdered, his only goal was to help keep us alive through the winter and get us into a partisan unit. He achieved that and so he was ready to die. But now what will happen to us? Will Popov kick us out of the camp? After all, we were accepted only because of Uncle Hershel's skills as a scout. With him gone, why would they continue to shelter and feed us?*

There was little need for worry. The Shainwalds had already proven their worth.

In late June, the battalion took in a small band of independent partisans, almost all young Jews. Some in the group had escaped from the Luboml ghetto with Meir and had carried out hit-and-run attacks on the enemy for months.

Beila noticed that one of them was wearing Meir's jacket. When pressed for an explanation, the partisan hesitated to tell the Shainwalds the horrible truth: Meir was killed in a firefight with the Germans.

Sonia felt her knees go weak and her stomach churn. *Meir, the liveliest one of us all, the one who made us laugh, the one who had the best chance of surviving, is gone!* She wanted to throw herself on the ground and weep, but she and her grief-stricken parents were once again forced to hold their emotions in check. They even were ordered to stick to their routine and complete the day's work assignments as if nothing had happened. Finally, when they were able to retreat to their tent, Sonia and her parents collapsed in heartache and cried themselves to sleep.

With her youngest son killed so soon after the death of her beloved brother and only a year after her firstborn's probable death, Beila barely had the will to live. She was so depressed that she didn't speak for days, which deeply worried Sonia, who was mired in her own grief and yearned for her mother's support. "*Mameh*, I am your child, too, and I need you," Sonia told her. Beila understood and found the strength to carry on.

To ease her heartache, Sonia threw herself into her work as an assistant to a bighearted Russian Jewish doctor, helping treat the wounded and the sick. Because there was a chronic shortage of medicine, they usually tried to use herbal remedies.

In early 1944, the Fyodorov brigade joined forces with the regular Red Army to confront the Wehrmacht in the Ukrainian city of Kovel. Partisans harassed the Germans from the rear while the Soviets attacked from the front. Joining hundreds of reinforcements from the brigade, Sonia left the security of their camp for the battle zone.

For the next ten days, she and the doctor worked nonstop in the most severe test of physical and mental stamina she would ever experience. Desperately trying to save lives and comfort the dying, they toiled in a Spartan field clinic in a birch grove near the battlefield. Because the trees were bare, the clinic was exposed from above and made a tempting target for enemy fighter planes that strafed the area.

Explosions of nearby mortar rounds constantly shook the field clinic. The deafening combat noise—a relentless barrage of grenades, cannons, and rockets—rattled Sonia's nerves. *Any minute now, we could be blasted to bits or overrun by German troops,* she thought. But she couldn't worry about her own life. She knew that if she wanted to help, she had to stay focused on saving the lives of others.

Day and night the injured were brought into the field clinic by the wagonload: blown-off limbs, punctured organs, gaping chest wounds. Worst of all, there was little that Sonia and the doctor could do. Drugs and supplies ran out so fast that it became difficult to perform any medical procedure without spreading infection. With no other options available to her, Sonia used the same bandages repeatedly, taking them off those who died and putting them on the next group of wounded.

Sometimes all she could provide were words of comfort to those who couldn't be saved. "Soon, soon, your suffering will stop," she would murmur. Many of the brigade's best fighters died right before her eyes as she held their limp hands.

Every day seemed worse than the previous one. Sonia barely slept and didn't wash, change her clothes, or remove her shoes during the entire ten-day shift. Lighting a fire would have given their position away, so they lacked hot food and sustained themselves with nothing more than rations of crackers and dried bread.

Finally, after a week and a half of fierce fighting, both sides temporarily backed off to regroup. During the lull in a battle that would last two bloody months, the exhausted teenager returned to the partisan camp. Her parents, who had been frantic about the fate of their daughter, didn't even recognize her at first because her hair was matted and tangled from sweat, her face was drawn from fatigue and caked in dirt, and her clothes were covered in the dried blood of the wounded. But once they realized it was really Sonia, they were overjoyed to see her.

Having proven herself in the battle at Kovel, Sonia was given more responsibility as well as a horse, which she rode bareback. She often accompanied a reconnaissance squad that fought in skirmishes with the Bulbutzye. One time she was assigned to Piotr's unit.

Usually, though, they wouldn't see each other for several days at a time because he went on lengthy missions. But Sonia was never far from his mind. Piotr penned many love poems when he was out on patrol and had them delivered to her by a comrade who was returning to camp. In one of his poems, he wrote, "Without words you let me understand that you fell in love with me in the same way I did with you." Like all partisans, including Sonia, he was always aware that each day might be the last, so he tried to live it to the fullest as best he could under the difficult circumstances. And so he wrote to Sonia, "Take all . . . while the heart still breathes."

Sonia knew only too well that death was a partisan's constant companion.

One day, Sonia was on a mission with a reconnaissance unit when they rested in a clearing. Before riding out with a smaller team to scout the area, the leader of the mission, who was an officer from Piotr's hometown of Vitebsk, Belorussia, took Sonia aside. He handed her a leather pouch containing detailed maps and charts, personal letters, photographs, and messages he wanted sent to his family in case he died. "A few of us are going to see what's out there," he told her. "You stay here and if I don't return, make sure all these things go to the right places—and let my mother know how I died."

Hours later, he was killed in an ambush by Bulbutzye who were disguised as friendly Russian soldiers. Only one member of the team survived the attack.

By spring 1944, the Germans were reeling from repeated defeats at the hands of the Red Army. Sonia and her comrades were feeling optimistic that the fighting in their region would soon be over for good. For the first time in years, she began dreaming of a new life, possibly as Piotr's wife, and settling down in a comfy home and raising children.

But war cares nothing about hopes and dreams and love. Piotr Menaker—the one person she was closest to other than her parents—was killed on a reconnaissance mission. The gut-wrenching shock hit Sonia hard, but she couldn't properly mourn his death because of the partisans' code of showing no emotion. And for that policy, she was angry at them. *I should have the right to grieve! I should be allowed to wallow in my own loss! I feel so empty without him.*

Just days after Piotr's death, the region was secured by the Red Army. For Sonia, liberation was bittersweet. Although relieved that combat had ceased, she was heartsick that she couldn't share this happy moment with Piotr.

With the fighting in the region over, the brigade was disbanded. Before the Shainwalds left, they participated with their comrades in a ceremony marking the end of the partisans' service. Gathered in an open field with flags flapping in the breeze, they heard a senior Red Army official thank everyone for their sacrifices.

Sonia felt a new sense of freedom, but it wasn't the same as someone who had survived a concentration camp or had emerged from hiding. That's because she had already felt liberated ever since her first day as a partisan.

═══

*Shortly after leaving the partisans, Beila died from typhus. Then Sonia fell ill with the same deadly disease, but ultimately recovered.*

*Later that summer, she and her father, Wolf, returned to Luboml with their heads held high from their service as partisans. But the destruction of the town, the Jewish community, and nearly all of her loved ones blotted out any feelings of triumph. Ninety-nine percent of Luboml's Jews were murdered by Germans and their local henchmen. The Great Synagogue, which had been used as a stable by the Nazis, had been demolished by the Russians.*

*With the town now under Soviet control, Sonia*

became deputy director of the post office and Wolf headed a government-run fur and hide business. They reunited with Tichon and his wife, Fedora. As a token of gratitude for keeping the Shainwalds and Hershel alive in the forest, Wolf gave the couple Hershel's furniture.

For Sonia, remaining in Luboml was like living in a cemetery. It tore her up to see the site of her family home at 37 Chelmska Street, which had turned into a vacant lot full of overgrown weeds. Murderers, looters, and fire had taken everything away. All that remained was that one stone step, where she stood often and wept.

In 1945 Sonia and her father moved to Chełm, Poland, where Sonia fell in love with businessman Isaak Orbuch, a Polish-born Jew who was a former soldier. They married later that year and so did her father, who wed a widowed Holocaust survivor who had been hidden by a non-Jewish family during the war.

Bribing a Russian soldier, the four of them were smuggled out of Poland to the American-occupied sector of Berlin, Germany. From there, they lived in the Zeilsheim displaced persons camp where, less than two years later, Sonia gave birth to a daughter, Bella. In 1949 they all immigrated to the United States, where Isaak became a successful businessman in commercial real estate in New York. In 1951 their son, Paul, was born.

While tending to family and business, the Orbuchs

were active in raising and donating money for several Jewish causes. In 1960 Isaak was diagnosed with Parkinson's disease, a neurological condition that slowly robbed him of his life. But despite his illness, the couple continued to travel and do their charity work for many years. Isaak died in 1997. By then they had moved to Marin County, California, where Sonia, a grandmother, lives today.

In the late 1990s, she tried to contact Tichon. Sonia learned that the Soviet government had imprisoned him from 1951 until his death ten years later for his political beliefs. Swayed by Sonia's written testimony, Yad Vashem, a Jerusalem-based Jewish organization, posthumously honored Tichon as one of the Righteous Among the Nations, an award given to gentiles who risked their lives to save Jews.

Says Sonia, "There's a saying that fits my life in America: 'The past is never dead and buried. It isn't even past.' I've lived sixty years in the New World, but in many ways, I've never left the Old. Every day my heart aches from the loss of my mother and two brothers, dozens of other relatives, and nearly all of my childhood friends. I've keenly felt their absence at every stage of my adult life: in times of joy when I married and had children, in times of sadness when I grappled with my husband's illness and death. . . . I never visited Luboml after immigrating to America. I knew that no Jews remained *there, and I simply couldn't bear to set foot on those blood-soaked streets again."*

*Sonia has kept two of Piotr's poems—the only items from the forest still in her possession. "They are precious to me, and I have read them again and again in private moments during all the years that have passed," she says. "At one point I worried that the penciled script might fade, so I went over every word in my own hand. That he loved and protected me in the wilderness gave me comfort and strength later in my life."*

You can read a more detailed account of Sonia Shainwald Orbuch's experiences as a partisan in her book, *Here, There Are No Sarahs* (RDR Books and the Judah L. Magnes Museum).

## "IF ANYONE KILLS A JEW, HE WILL BE KILLED"
# FRANK BLAICHMAN

WAR SEEMED SO FAR away for young Frank Blaichman.

With no radio and no talk of politics in the four-room apartment he shared with his parents and six siblings, he had no clue how his life and everyone else's in Poland was about to drastically change—or tragically end.

Growing up in the quiet town of Kamionka in eastern Poland at a time when horses pulled wagons and people read by candlelight, Frank focused on his studies at school and having fun with his friends. The slightly built teenager often played with his pals in the nearby Bratnik forest, sometimes picking blueberries and mushrooms for the family. He was always riding his bike, except in the winter when he was gliding over ice on skates fashioned out of old sickles.

Even when Germany invaded Poland on September 1, 1939, the 16-year-old assumed life would go on as usual, although he did notice the grave concern etched on the faces of his mother, Ita, and his father, Chaim, a grain dealer.

But then, weeks after the invasion, refugees fleeing from the advancing enemy streamed through Kamionka. They came on foot and bicycle and by horse-drawn wagons, hoping to reach Russian-occupied territory to the east, where they felt safer. Frank started worrying only after he saw Polish soldiers arriving in town in full retreat, tossing away their rifles in panic or trading their weapons for civilian clothes.

In early October, the first wave of German soldiers showed up and immediately began persecuting many of the town's 200 Jewish families. Within days after the troops' arrival, Frank witnessed brutality for the first time. From a safe distance, he watched soldiers force a group of Jewish men to dig ditches. The soldiers struck them with rifle butts, cursed them, and laughed at them. When the Jews were worn out from digging deep trenches, the soldiers ordered them to shovel all the dirt back in the ditches again. All the while, the beatings never stopped. Shaken by what he saw, Frank could only fantasize that one day he would get even with the Germans.

As the months dragged on, life became worse for the Jews. If a Jew failed to salute any person of authority, he was often punched or slapped for being disrespectful; and if he did salute, he sometimes was struck and told, "You're not human enough to salute a German!"

Nazis burst into homes and kidnapped those they

thought might organize a resistance movement—teachers, rabbis, and intellectuals such as Frank's uncle, Mayer Lewin. They were whisked away to the Majdanek concentration camp in nearby Lublin. Frank never saw him or the others again.

At any time of the day or night, Nazis conducted unannounced roundups of able-bodied Jews and forced them to work as slave laborers in occupied estates around Kamionka. Whole families disappeared in other abductions, terrorizing the community because no one knew who would vanish next.

Jews were executed for the slightest infraction. Uncle Moishe was shot to death after police found meat he was preparing for a holy day. Cousin Brucha was murdered in her bed for the crime of possessing fresh bread.

Perplexed why no one seemed to be resisting, Frank asked the Jewish elders in the synagogue, "Why do they want to kill us?"

"Our only crime is that we are Jews."

"Why don't we do something about this?" he pressed them.

"With God's help, we will overcome these difficult times," replied one elder. "If God wills otherwise, then we must accept our fate."

"Why not get weapons to fight back?" Frank asked.

"In Warsaw and other cities, for every German who's killed, they kill one hundred Jews," came the answer. "So even if we had weapons, we couldn't use them because it could cause the death of hundreds of our fellow Jews."

"Well, I can't just wait to be picked up and killed," Frank declared. "I'm going to escape."

"And go where?"

"To the forest if I have to," he said. "I'm going to stay in the area and figure out what to do."

"The Jew-haters will find you and kill you. And if they don't, the winter will."

"I will not be captured," Frank proclaimed.

When the Germans began rationing food, Frank found a way to bring produce and meat into town. His grandmother ran a small general store, so she supplied him with goods such as tobacco and yarn, which he put in the baskets on his bike. He rode out to nearby villages and farms and traded the goods for food. He passed himself off as a gentile by keeping the Star of David armband at home.

In October 1942, the Nazis announced that within 24 hours Jews would be moved to a big ghetto in the nearby town of Lubartow. That evening, Frank told his parents, "I'm not going. I cannot and will not live and die in a ghetto."

They understood. Because of their religious beliefs and need to care for their children, they chose to stay in the ghetto.

Before leaving, Frank stared into his parents' eyes and knew they were thinking the same thing he was: When will we see each other again? As much as they wanted to cry and hug, they stifled the urge for the sake of the other children who didn't know this was good-bye—probably forever. "Maybe I'll see you in Lubartow," mumbled Frank, fighting hard to suppress his emotions. Stuffing a small loaf of bread in his pocket, he walked out.

He spent the night with friends, hiding out on an estate. The next day they joined up with about 30 Jews who had slipped out of Kamionka. After a lengthy debate about what to do next, they decided that maybe it was best after all to go to the ghetto in Lubartow. One of the Jews summed it up, "We have no chance of surviving the winter in the forest, and you can't trust farmers to help us because most of them hate Jews. We're better off in the ghetto."

Frank reluctantly agreed. But as they neared Lubartow, he had a change of heart. Spotting a cross on top of the big church that overlooked the town, he stopped dead in his tracks as though blocked by an invisible force. His inner voice warned him, *You promised you would never go freely into a ghetto, and yet that's where you're going.*

"I just can't take another step toward Lubartow," he told his friends. He wished the others well and headed off in a different direction. But with each step, his confidence began to fade and he felt overwhelmed, terrified, and alone. Frank was troubled with second thoughts: *Have I done the right thing? Have I abandoned my family? Could I have done anything for them? How much longer could I have hoped to live if I had stayed with them?*

As he wrestled with questions too weighty for any teenager to bear, it started to rain and he started to cry. Drenched and drained, he finally pulled himself together with the help of one simple but powerful thought: *I'm still free.*

He hiked toward the farm of Alexsander and Alfreda Klos, kindhearted gentiles who had done business with him and his grandmother. They had told him earlier he could hide out with them. When he arrived, they and their two children greeted him warmly. The couple gave him comfort, food, and a place to sleep even though they knew that if the Germans found out, the whole family would be killed.

The next day, Mr. Klos told Frank, "I have some bad news. All the Jews who were deported to Lubartow were not put in the ghetto. The Germans took them away by train to an unknown destination."

The anguish that Frank felt nearly paralyzed him because "unknown destination" meant a concentration camp. When he gathered his thoughts, he wiped the tears from his eyes and murmured, "I'll never see my family again."

He eventually joined a group of weary Jewish families, about 100 people of all ages, who were hiding out in bunkers they had dug in the Bratnik forest. Although he was among the youngest, Skinny Frank (Suchy Franek, as he was called in Yiddish) often gave advice to the adults. He showed them how to reduce their campfire smoke—which could give their location away to the enemy—by using dry wood instead of green wood and by stringing blankets a few feet above the flames. He also formed a defense unit of fellow teenagers to protect the group from roving gangs of hoodlums who lurked in the woods looking for Jews to assault. Because he knew the area so well, Frank told them the best villages and farmhouses to visit for food and supplies.

But it was getting increasingly dangerous. Either out of anti-Semitism or fear the Germans would kill them for cooperating with Jews, many peasants chased Frank and his comrades away.

The Jews had no weapons to defend themselves or to convince villagers to help them. So they stole pitchforks from neighboring farms and had a supportive blacksmith remove all the tines of each tool except the middle one, which he shortened and straightened. Then he attached a shoulder strap to each handle. From a distance or at dusk, each pitchfork looked like a rifle with a bayonet. If a farmer was reluctant to sell food to the Jews, Frank made sure the person saw the "armed men" who were walking back and forth nearby. The ruse often made the farmer change his mind. After buying the food, Frank would hand over a receipt so the farmer could prove to the Germans that he was forced at gunpoint to give food to the Jews.

Because the Nazis had taken away the Jews' businesses, homes, and possessions, many in the group assumed they would not be harassed in the forest. As a result, they sometimes acted carelessly, like the time in November when several young women walked into a village in broad daylight. Frank was furious, worried that an informer would follow them back and discover the campsite. "I don't intend to be captured and killed just because some of our women refuse to abide by the rules," he told the leaders.

So Frank and other members of his defense unit moved to the edge of the forest and built their own bunker and cooked their own meals. They agreed to help guard the area but they would be independent of the larger group.

Near dawn three days after moving into their own bunker, they heard gunfire and explosions erupting from the main camp. "Germans!" Frank and his comrades fled farther into the forest, crawled across a road guarded by a three-man machine-gun squad, ran for another hour, and then hid in a thorny thicket until midnight.

When they returned to the main camp, they were

sickened by the sight. Every bunker had been blown up and bodies were scattered all over. "They didn't stand a chance," muttered Frank. He and his comrades buried the victims and then said Kaddish. "I swear we will avenge the deaths of our friends."

About a dozen had survived the attack by fleeing. Of the 100 Jews in the group, now only 25 were left.

"It's too dangerous to establish a fixed campsite," Frank told the others. "It's better if we keep on the move. We shouldn't spend more than one night in the same place, and never remain in the same spot for more than an hour or two during the day."

For weeks in the bitterly cold winter, they slogged through the snow and sleet and slept on frozen ground and under pine trees. They stole potatoes from big estates and cooked them over open fires. There was no sense complaining. At least they were alive.

To get arms, Frank spent a day bullying farmers into giving up caches of weapons they had collected when the Polish soldiers were retreating. He did it by pretending to be a Russian paratrooper who had been ordered to organize a partisan unit. He sported a mustache to look older and wore a policeman's sheepskin-lined blue overcoat—a gift from a farmer who had donated coats, hats, and uniforms thrown away during the retreat. Frank pinned a badge on his lapel to make himself look official and also carried a rusty old pistol that didn't work.

Backed by his comrades who were carrying their fake rifles, Frank conned farmers into believing his lie. At the end of the day, Frank and his men had eight working weapons. "Finally we can defend ourselves!" he exclaimed. "We can call ourselves partisans!"

Those in Frank's group who had been in the military taught the rest how to use the weapons. After a week of target practice, Frank came close to hitting the bull's-eye every time. The group obtained four more weapons, so a dozen men were now armed and could help protect the other 13 members, which included 2 young women and 11 older men who couldn't fight because of health issues or religious beliefs.

Two weeks later while in the woods, the partisans watched three young Polish men who appeared to be gathering mushrooms. "Something isn't right," whispered Frank. When two of them got close enough, the partisans jumped them. The third man ran off, shouting, "Jews! Jews!" They disarmed the two Poles, whose pistols were tucked in their belts, and tied their hands and stuffed rags in their mouths.

Suddenly, the forest reverberated with gunfire from German troops. Grabbing their two captives, the partisans fled to the safety of a friendly farmer's barn where Frank, with the help of two comrades, interrogated one of the Poles.

"What were you doing out there?" Frank demanded.

"Looking for mushrooms."

"In the middle of winter?" When the Pole mumbled something that made no sense, Frank put his gun to the man's head and said, "If you don't start talking, I'll shoot you."

"The Germans recruited us about seven months ago," the Pole blurted. "Our job was to go into villages around Kamionka and warn the people that they would be severely punished if they helped Jews."

Frank waved his gun in front of the Pole's face and said, "What else?"

"We recruited young men to hunt down and capture Jews and bring them to us. If we found any valuables on a Jew, we'd take them and then kill him."

"Did you have anything to do with the attack on the bunker site?"

The Pole hesitated before nodding. "Yes, my partner and I followed the girls from the village and spotted the camp. Then we led the Germans to the site."

"And what were you doing out there today?"

"We were sent by the Germans to catch any Jews who might have survived the attack."

"Did you ever think you would be captured by Jews?"

"No, never. I always felt protected by the German might. Besides, no Jew had ever resisted me or my partner before."

Then Frank grilled the other Pole and got similar answers.

After the Poles revealed that the Germans had a vast network of informers, the partisans took the two captives to several villages and forced them to point out the collaborators. Six of them were taken prisoner and brought back to the forest.

"We're going to send a message that those who help Germans murder Jews will be tracked down and killed," Frank told the prisoners. "We're going to make good on our promise to avenge the deaths of our families."

There was no shortage of volunteers to carry out the execution of all eight collaborators.

In the dead of winter, Frank and his comrades began spending the nights in farmhouses and barns. For safety reasons, half the group would sleep inside the farmhouse while the other half stayed in the barn.

They spent one night at the home of Boleslaw Dabrowski, a caring farmer in the village of Staroscin. Early the next morning Frank and his cousin Froim headed out to meet with the leader of another partisan group. About a mile from the house, the two began hearing gunfire and seeing smoke coming from Staroscin. Stopping a farmer who was traveling in his sleigh from the village, they asked him what had happened.

"It's terrible," he replied. "German soldiers surrounded the Dabrowski house and set it on fire. Anyone who rushed out was gunned down."

The partisans in the barn had escaped and so had four others, who had been in the house. But six comrades, including the two young women, as well as five Dabrowski family members, had either been shot or burned to death. Only Mrs. Dabrowski was spared.

The partisans concluded that Polish informers had trailed them to the house and alerted the Germans. From then on, whenever the unit moved, one man would drop off to the side and remain hidden, watching to see if they were being followed. To throw off potential trackers, the group zigzagged through the fields and sometimes circled back.

Despite the precautions, they were ambushed shortly after the Dabrowski tragedy. After a 15-minute firefight, the partisans chased their attackers, killing two and capturing two others, who turned out to be teenagers.

Under harsh questioning, the prisoners confessed they were members of the anti-Semitic Home Army—an armed force of one of Poland's political parties—and gave up the names of several local leaders. "We had been ordered to kill you because you're Jews," said one. "Our leaders said that no

Jew should be allowed to survive the war. Are you going to kill us?"

After discussing the captives' fate with his comrades, Frank told the two punks, "We'll let you go because you're so young, you've given us valuable information, and none of us was wounded. Even though we live in a world where there's no justice for Jews, we try to be just. But if anyone kills a Jew, he will be killed. If anyone beats a Jew, he will be beaten. You have been warned. Don't let us catch you again."

Frank and his young comrades were growing into their new lives as partisans. Many, like him, had entered the forest as boys with no experience of living in the wild, of stealing food to stay alive, or of killing another human being. Except for those who had served in the military, they had never even held a weapon. From teenage fugitives on the run, they were now an all-Jewish independent guerrilla force that tracked down—and, in many cases, executed—spies and collaborators. The group also began carrying out joint operations with anti-Nazi organizations. In addition, the unit made arrangements for wounded partisans and Jews who couldn't defend themselves to stay with compassionate farmers and peasants.

Soon Frank and his men teamed up with another partisan unit, which grew when they were joined by a small band of former soldiers who had escaped from the POW camp in

Lublin. Together, the group was now 60 men strong.

One day, villagers informed Frank that two strangers had showed up, asking how to join the partisans. Frank agreed to meet them near the edge of the woods, but he had his comrades hide close by in case of trouble.

The men told Frank how eager they were to join his group and how much they hated the Germans.

"There are many different partisan groups in the region, almost all non-Jewish. Why would gentiles like you want to join up with a group of Jews?"

Both men stammered, unable to come up with a believable answer. On Frank's signal, the partisans dashed from their hidden positions and disarmed the men. Under interrogation, the men confessed they were working for the Germans. A committee of six partisans, who served as judge and jury in matters like this, sentenced them to death. Time and again, Frank and his men unmasked spies trying to infiltrate their group. The spies all met the same fate as the first two.

During the summer, Frank learned that four Jewish men who had escaped from a labor camp in Lublin had been murdered by thugs in a nearby village. The Jews had been hiding in the home of a villager, but when they ran out of money, he threw them out. They were captured by local hoodlums who marched them through the village, cursing and spitting on them, before they were clubbed to death in front of everyone.

Along with Geniek Kaminsky, who was a member of the People's Guard (an armed anti-Nazi organization of Polish citizens), Frank and his men gathered the villagers in the town square. Then Kaminsky delivered a powerful speech, condemning the murders and urging the people to help all Jews. "Don't you realize that the enemy of the Jews is also the enemy of the Polish people?" Kaminsky told them. "First, Jews are treated like dogs. And then the Poles will be next. Decent human beings do not club other people to death."

When Kaminsky was finished, the partisans asked the peasants to point out the killers, which they did. The murderers were taken away by members of the People's Guard and executed. Before leaving the village, Kaminsky told the peasants, "The partisans and the People's Guard will protect any Jew in hiding, and we will punish anyone who victimizes Jews."

As more German troops moved into the area on their way to the eastern front to fight the Russians, the partisans stepped up their efforts to attack and destroy enemy supply lines. Frank and his men targeted convoys led by motorcycles with sidecars that held machine gunners, because those motorcycles were used only when trucks were transporting vital supplies.

The partisans staked out positions in drainage ditches along the road, spreading out about 200 feet apart in groups of eight to ten men. The first group's job was to take out the machine gunners in the lead motorcycles. When the trucks behind them slowed down, the partisans blasted the convoy with machine-gun fire and antitank rockets, aiming at the gas tanks so the trucks would explode. Each convoy was left in a tangled mass of burning metal and billowing smoke.

One night, Frank and his men, now numbering nearly 100, returned to Kamionka on a bittersweet mission—to burn down the synagogue in the town square. As a deliberate insult to Jews, the Nazis were using the synagogue for their offices. The Jewish partisans felt it was better to have their house of worship destroyed than to have it degraded every day by the local German command.

Under cover of darkness, the men sneaked up to the synagogue, but German soldiers stationed on the roof of the nearby school spotted them and began shooting. The partisans returned fire. Meanwhile, several busted into the building, poured gasoline on the wooden floors and file cabinets, and set it all on fire.

In April 1944, Frank's unit joined forces with Jewish partisans headed by Chiel Grynszpan to bolster the People's Army, a Polish partisan group. Frank was promoted to first lieutenant and made a platoon commander.

They soon engaged the German soldiers in a fierce battle. Afterward, Frank and his men led columns of fighters during the night to a village south of Amelin. Acting as the guide for the other commanders, Frank deployed the men in farmhouses and barns and in camps in the woods. He fell asleep on the floor of a house for a few hours until he was awakened by Lonka Pfefferkorn, the partisans' most reliable scout, who rode up on horseback. He handed Frank a written order to set up an ambush of German troops who were approaching from Lublin.

Suddenly the two heard an enemy plane flying low overhead. Machine-gun fire ripped through the roof and into the floor only three feet away from Frank, shattering the floorboards and spewing splinters in all directions. Half-dressed, he grabbed his machine gun and raced outside with Pfefferkorn to see five planes from the Luftwaffe circling the village. As other partisans dashed into the woods, the planes attacked them. Zooming so low they nearly scraped the treetops, the planes bombed and strafed the area.

Then German troops stormed the partisans' position. While his comrades put up a sturdy defense, Frank dashed back and forth along the front line, firing at the enemy and making sure the machine-gun loaders had enough ammo. He had never experienced such a ferocious fight before.

During the battle, Frank heard a gut-wrenching scream

and saw a fellow partisan named Romek fall. Shrapnel from a bomb had blown out his hip and left him bleeding to death. As Romek lay in agony, Frank sent for a medic, but there was nothing anyone could do to save him.

"We have to do something!" Frank shouted. "We can't let him suffer like this!"

"I know," said partisan Jan Wojtovitcz. He lifted his rifle and aimed it at Romek's head. Frank couldn't look. He knew shooting a dying comrade who could not be helped was far more humane than letting him suffer excruciating pain. He wished he could have grieved, said Kaddish, and talked about what a valiant fighter and fine human being Romek was. But there was no time; the battle was intensifying.

Wave after wave of German troops tried to break through the defensive lines, but the partisans courageously held their positions throughout the day until nightfall when the Germans finally pulled back. The enemy had suffered hundreds of casualties while the partisans lost 30 men and had 25 wounded. Soon hundreds of German reinforcements, including tank columns, approached the area. Realizing they would be outmanned, the partisans moved out to avoid further bloodshed.

About a week later, Frank and his men met up with Chiel Grynszpan's group in the village of Kodeniec. It was there where Frank met shy, beautiful 18-year-old Cesia Pomeranc, one of the women who cooked, washed, and performed other support duties for Grynszpan's group.

Cesia told Frank that when she was 16, the Nazis deported her entire family of nine to work as slave laborers on an estate in Adampol. While her father toiled in the stables, Cesia, five of her siblings, and her mother worked in the fields harvesting fruit and potatoes. The head of the camp made her youngest brother, Abie, the camp mascot.

Her brother Janek escaped and joined several relatives and acquaintances who were hiding out in the woods. Then Cesia and another brother, Jurek, sneaked out of the labor camp and reunited with Janek. Her parents and the rest of her siblings were supposed to join them in a few days once her father obtained some weapons. But they never showed.

"We heard that the Germans had taken the Jewish families to the edge of a pit in Adampol and shot them all," Cesia told Frank. "The Germans checked to make sure everyone in the pit was dead and then left. But Abie was small and the bullets missed him. He fell into the pit with the rest and lay there all day and then crawled out and ran into the woods crying until a Polish farmer found him. A few days later, the farmer came to our campsite with Abie and asked if anyone recognized him. We couldn't believe it. Our little brother was alive!"

She said that shortly after their reunion, Janek and Jurek

went into a village to get bread, but on their way back, Janek was shot in the side. Jurek helped him get back to the camp. "When I saw how much blood Janek was losing, I ripped apart a linen shirt and put some threads in the bullet hole to serve as a dressing," Cesia recalled. "He was conscious but looked as if he was dying. After two days, Jurek and I carried him through the forest until we found a camp of partisans. Some Russian partisans took Janek away for medical treatment, and I didn't see him for two years. He spent all that time with a Russian partisan unit while Jurek, Abie, and I ended up with Chiel Grynszpan's group."

When Frank heard Cesia's story, he thought of his own sisters and offered to protect her and Abie if she cooked for him and two other leaders in his group. He was extremely pleased when she agreed.

By summer 1944, the entire Parczew forest area had become a giant camp for partisans, now numbering in the thousands. With the help of Russian airdrops of arms and paratroopers, the partisans were winning battles with the Germans and destroying enemy supply and troop trains. As a result, the German command mobilized a large force, including three Waffen-SS battalions, to rid the forest of partisans. Meanwhile, the Red Army kept advancing from the east.

One night in late July, Frank lost contact with his

comrades and ended up walking alone in a field during a heavy downpour. The next morning he encountered a peasant who brought him bread, butter, cheese, and milk. "I heard something good," said the peasant. "The Russian army is only a few kilometers away."

*But that means the retreating Germans are near, too,* Frank thought. Remaining alert for signs of the approaching enemy, he sat down to eat his breakfast. Suddenly artillery shells began exploding all around him. One shell landed so close in the rain-soaked ground that it splashed mud all over him and left a big crater. He was pleased the rounds were from Russian artillery, but he was worried that he would become a casualty of friendly fire, so he sprinted to one of the first craters, hoping he would be safer there. He figured that if the artillerymen had adjusted their aim toward the German retreat, then no more rounds would land where he stood. But that was a big if. Wet, dirty, and tired, Frank thought that his luck might be running out. Fortunately, the range and direction of the rounds changed toward the German retreat.

Later that day, he rejoined his comrades outside a village on the Parczew forest. While looking through his binoculars, he saw camouflaged tanks in the distance and wondered, *Friend or foe?* He was still trying to make that determination when he spotted a figure on horseback riding toward him. The rider was wearing a military cap with a red band around it. That meant he was a Russian officer and that the tanks were Russian. *The worst is over,* thought Frank. *We have survived!*

≡

*Although the war in Europe lasted another ten months, Frank Blaichman no longer fought as a partisan. Instead, he was assigned to a unit of the Polish Security Police responsible for hunting down and investigating Nazi collaborators in Russian-occupied territory. In his job, he read many official reports of anti-Semitic gangs killing returning Jews and even throwing them off trains.*

*After the war, he asked for and received a discharge, and on September 6, 1945, he married Cesia. Because Poland was then a communist country, the couple couldn't leave legally. So they left all their worldly possessions behind and, with only the clothes on their backs, were smuggled to Germany by hiding under bags of letters in the back of a mail truck. Once they settled in Germany, Frank made a good living buying and selling goods on the black market. During this time, Cesia gave birth to their daughter, Bella Ita, named after her two grandmothers. The couple would later have a son, Charles.*

*In 1951 the family immigrated to New York City, where Frank became an American citizen and* an extremely successful builder, developer, and noted philanthropist.

"I have often wondered why I survived when so many didn't," Frank once wrote. "I have no answer. As a partisan, I was involved in many battles, with close fire coming at me from all sides. My friends and comrades, good men who had wanted nothing more than the opportunity to lead a simple life in the manner of their ancestors in Poland, died all around me. I wasn't really afraid during those times, maybe because I never thought about dying or surviving at all. My focus was on what I could do at any given moment against the enemy. Revenge had become my way of life."

In the 1960s, Frank and several other former partisans created the Federation of Former Jewish Underground Fighters Against Nazism to honor Jews who fought back. He later helped form a committee that raised money for a monument to partisans at Yad Vashem in Jerusalem. The monument is made up of six hexagonal granite blocks, each memorializing a million Jews killed in the Holocaust. The blocks are placed so the open space in the center forms the Star of David.

At the dedication of the memorial in 1985, Frank said, "History had placed on us the task of avenging the blood of our families and millions of our people who were brutally murdered by the Nazis. I remember those

*comrades—the courageous, brave men and women who,*
*together with us, answered the call of history to defend*
*Jewish lives, Jewish honor, and Jewish dignity. We are*
*the fortunate ones. We are the survivors who must and*
*will keep this legacy alive for generations to come."*

You can read a more detailed account of Frank Blaichman's experiences as a Jewish partisan in his book, *Rather Die Fighting* (Arcade Publishing).

# "I'LL FINALLY GET MY REVENGE FOR WHAT THEY DID TO MY FAMILY"
# MARTIN FRIEDMAN

MARTIN FRIEDMAN WAS LIVING a lie.

Appearing as a pious young Catholic, he lived and worked in a monastery. It was the only way a Jew like him could survive the murderous madness swirling throughout Czechoslovakia.

His parents, three of his six brothers, his only sister, her husband, and their infant daughter had been murdered in Auschwitz, the notorious Nazi death camp. His friends were either dead or half-starved in miserable slave labor camps like the one he had escaped from in Sered, Slovakia. In his hometown of Bánovce, his former neighbors, who had always been accepting and friendly toward his family, now despised and persecuted Jews.

And so in the summer of 1943, 17-year-old Martin hid in the monastery of the Order of Brothers of Mercy, protected by a carefully constructed illusion of faith and devotion to Catholicism. The sprawling monastery, which was nestled in the Tatra Mountains, was the home and spiritual center for ten monks who assumed the young man was a good Catholic because he attended Mass and worked for only room and board. Only one monk, 20-year-old Brother Rudolph, knew Martin was a Jew.

Martin felt safe inside the confines of the 20-foot-tall fieldstone walls where he tended to the fields and the gardens. He was grateful he had his own room, even if it was only a sparse cell that contained a bed with a straw mattress, a small table, and a couple of chairs. Martin seldom ventured outside its walls because the streets were too dangerous. Someone might discover he was a Jew.

As a quiet, mild-mannered young man, he blended in with the dozen townspeople who worked at the monastery as maids, cooks, farm laborers, and gardeners. Some were also caregivers to the 30 mentally and physically disabled patients who were housed in an infirmary in one corner of the monastery. The infirmary was a source of resentment for most of the pro-Nazi villagers, who wanted all the patients—especially the ten Jewish ones—sent to a concentration camp. But the monks refused, because they had made a moral commitment to keep the patients isolated and safe from a world that did not accept them.

Martin certainly could identify with the patients. Every day he remained on edge, worried that someone would point him out as a Jew or an escapee from the Sered slave labor camp and have him shipped him off to his death in Auschwitz. The ongoing war preyed on his mind: *What if the Germans win?* But with each passing month, he was heartened by reports that the Germans were suffering major defeats on the eastern front. When working in the fields of the monastery, he sometimes put his ear to the ground and listened to the reverberation of artillery in battles that were 100 or more miles away. *Even if the Germans lose, they still have poisoned the minds of millions,* he thought.

One night in spring 1944, he was jolted awake by the angry shouts of a crowd outside the monastery walls. He peered from the window and saw hundreds of townspeople carrying torches and chanting, "Give us the Jews! Give us the Jews!"

*They're coming for me!* For the next few minutes, he was paralyzed by terror, unable to move or think. When he finally regained control, he sprinted over to the church, which was inside the monastery, and entered from a side door, looking for the one person he trusted—Brother Rudolph.

All the monks lived in separate cells on the church's wraparound second-floor balcony. But when he ran up the stairs, he discovered the main hallway was locked by an iron gate. In his panic, Martin shook the bars, calling out the monk's name.

Prior Kostolansky, the priest who headed the monastery,

woke up and sleepily walked over to the gate. Seeing Martin trembling with fear, he unlocked it and led him to Brother Rudolph's cell. On the way, the prior told Martin, "Calm yourself, my son. It's not you they've come for. It's the Jews." The prior shook his head and sighed. "Ah, these misguided townspeople. How filled with hate they are. They want to take away all our poor, sick brothers in the infirmary."

After the prior turned him over to Brother Rudolph and left, Martin blurted through clenched teeth, "Rudolph, they've come for the Jews! Please hide me!"

The monk handed him a black woolen robe with a cowl to cover up his head. "Put this on," Brother Rudolph told him. "They'll think you're one of us."

Martin and the monk then watched anxiously out the window that overlooked the street 30 feet below. Other monks watched in silence as the drama unfolded.

With the torches casting a reddish glow on their angry faces, the people began threatening to bash in the monastery gate. They were launching a charge when Prior Kostolansky opened the church's main door and stepped out onto the massive stone steps facing the gate. A sudden hush fell over the mob until one of the villagers shouted, "Give us the Jews, Prior! They are our enemies!"

In a calm but commanding voice, Prior Kostolansky told them, "We harbor no enemies here. Inside our walls are only the poor, broken children of God who have been given over to my protection. Anyone who wants them must first step across my dead body." He stood tall, his defiant eyes slowly scanning the crowd.

No one said a word. No one moved. The prior remained rooted to the steps, staring down the hundreds of incensed villagers. As if on cue, it started to rain, dampening the heated moment. Then slowly the throng broke into small groups and returned to their homes without uttering a sound. When the streets were empty again, the prior closed the church door and went back to his room.

"Well, Martin, it's all over," said Brother Rudolph. "Let's go to sleep."

*Sleep? I can't sleep.* Martin was struck by the contrast between the bold actions of the prior and the meekness of Rudolph and the other monks. He realized that the Nazis were literally getting away with murder because too many people were passive; too many were saying "Let's go to sleep" instead of "Let's fight back."

The fear he had felt suddenly transformed into a desire to rise up against the Nazis and resist them with all his heart and soul. *I can't stay here anymore or I'll end up just as passive as the monks and wait for fate to decide if I live or die. No, I must find a way to join the partisans.*

Weeks earlier he had picked up one of many leaflets lying

on the ground. It was a message from the partisans urging the people of Slovakia to revolt against the Nazis. He had heard rumors that the partisans were swooping down from the mountains, blowing up bridges and trains, and harassing the enemy before disappearing back into the high country.

He knew just the person who could help him make contact with the partisans. When Martin had been in the Sered slave labor camp, his friend Shany had told him about a man named Brontos, who worked for the underground in the town of Poprad, about 25 miles from the monastery. Brontos had connections with the partisans.

Martin stuffed his belongings in a backpack, said good-bye to Brother Rudolph, and left the monastery. Striding down a country road with a sense of purpose, Martin felt his confidence growing. But the next morning, his poise was shaken when he encountered a large Hitler Youth group singing pro-Nazi songs.

*Should I have left the safety of the monastery?* he wondered. *Will someone discover who I really am? Were those partisan leaflets fake and really a trap to catch Jews? If I ask the wrong person about the partisans, I'll end up in a concentration camp . . . or dead.*

But seeing the trees beginning to show buds, Martin thought how spring represented new life. *Now is the time of my rebirth. Now is the time to take action. Now is the time to fight for my future.* And once again he rediscovered his courage.

He soon reached Brontos's home in Poprad. Brontos, a kind man in his fifties, welcomed Martin, giving him food and a place to sleep. "Tell me. How is it that a young man like you wants to be a partisan?" Brontos asked.

"I lived with my family in Bánovce, and life was good until the Nazis came," Martin said. "I remember about this time five years ago everyone sat around the table for the Passover Seder [feast] and my father asked each of us to make one promise—that we would all be together again for the next Seder. We all gave a promise that we intended to keep. But . . ." He shook his head and his eyes watered. "Almost all of my family of ten have been murdered. I was *lucky,*" he said sarcastically. "I went to the labor camp in Sered. That's where I met our mutual friend, Shany. He was still alive when I last saw him. My brother Vilo was there, too."

"How badly are they treated there?" Brontos asked.

"Very bad. You work twelve hours a day six days a week and half a day Sunday. Many die from poor conditions and lack of decent food. Commander Vozar is an evil man. One day, he was riding around on his motorcycle, shooting at birds with his rifle. Then he started aiming at the prisoners, picking them off one at a time as if he was in his own personal shooting gallery. He didn't care. The Hlinka Guard is even more brutal than the Nazis. They have a license to kill. To them, Jews aren't human and, since the Jews will be exterminated anyway, it doesn't matter if they're brutalized."

"How did you escape?"

"I became very sick with a lung infection. The guards were afraid I'd infect others, so they sent me to the infirmary. They wanted me to get better because I was a good soccer player, and the Nazis liked watching matches between other prisoners. I was sent to a private sanitarium to recover and I met Brother Rudolph, who was a patient there. After he returned to the monastery, I just walked away from the sanitarium and hid for a year in the monastery. I felt pretty secure there, but I finally realized I couldn't stay. I must fight back."

Martin remained with Brontos for several days until Brontos obtained false papers for him. "Martin Petrasek is your new identity," Brontos said. "You must have a last name that has no connection with the Sered camp. And the documents say you are unacceptable for military service. That way, you can move around freely without fear of getting drafted. One other thing: Don't let anyone know you're Jewish."

Soon Martin and another partisan recruit, named Aloise, were standing at a crossroads waiting for a truck that would take them to a partisan unit. When the truck appeared, Martin gave the driver the password, "Regards from Wilhelm." Then the two jumped in the back, joining an intense-looking, unsmiling partisan named Franz.

As they jostled along a bumpy dirt road into the hills, Martin thought, *I'm going to be a partisan! I'll be fighting the Nazis instead of being shipped off to slaughter. I'll finally get my revenge for what they did to my family.*

During the ride, he remembered that he was carrying two sets of papers, one bearing his real name and the other the fake identity. Knowing how suspicious partisans were, he didn't want them to think he was a double spy. *I certainly don't need both sets. All my hiding is a thing of the past because now I'm free.* He took out his real papers and began ripping them up. *Martin Friedman no longer exists. I am Martin Petrasek!* Happily throwing pieces out of the truck, he was so caught up in the moment that he failed to notice Franz had ordered the driver to stop.

Unexpectedly, Franz cocked his gun and, at arm's length, aimed it at Martin's head. "Don't move!" he hissed.

"What's the matter with you?" Martin said.

"Why were you tearing up those papers?"

"I don't need them anymore. I'm a partisan now."

Turning to the driver, Franz said, "He's a spy. Let's shoot him now."

"My God! How can you say this?" Martin protested, his voice cracking with fear. "I'm one of you!" *This can't be happening to me!* He was stunned, angry, and frightened. All his efforts to reach this point, all the dangers he had overcome, and now it might end at the hands of the very people he wanted to join?

"He's a friend of Brontos," said Aloise. "You should at least check first to see if he really is a spy before you shoot him."

"Okay, we'll let the commander decide," said Franz. But he kept his gun trained on Martin throughout the ride and even after they left the truck and began hiking up a steep mountain path.

Martin arrived at the partisans' camp not as a recruit but as a prisoner. The camp, a flat area about 200 yards wide and 1,000 yards long, was rimmed by boulders and shaded by tall pine trees. About 300 partisans, some armed, were building shelters or training for battle.

He was brought before their leader, Captain Vorobiov, a Russian officer and former teacher in his late twenties, whose hard, intelligent eyes stared at Martin. After listening to Franz's allegations, Vorobiov told Martin, "We will keep you locked in a room until we learn the truth. It will take a few days."

Martin nodded and didn't say a word. He was fully aware that partisans were distrustful by nature. *They'll see I'm not a spy after they talk to Brontos. Everything will turn out fine. If I can't find a home with these people, then I might as well die.*

Three days later, the captain came into the room and pulled out a large-caliber handgun from his belt. Martin gasped. *He's going to shoot me right now!*

"Here, I want you to have it," said the captain, placing the weapon handle first into Martin's hand. "I'm sorry we detained you like this, but we had to be sure."

"I understand," said Martin, still recovering from the mistaken impression that he was about to be executed.

Pointing to the gun, the captain said, "It's loaded. Have you ever used one of these before?"

"Yes," lied Martin. Having never touched a gun before, he didn't know the proper way to hold it, let alone shoot it.

"Good. You will train with this gun and other weapons while we form a partisan army strong enough to liberate Czechoslovakia. Come. I'll show you around the camp."

They walked from bunker to bunker, each one a shelter carved out of the hillside or scooped out of the ground and covered with logs. They also went past framed shelters covered with branches. The captain introduced him to a band of 20 partisans—most of them bearded, dirty, and rugged—with whom he would live, train, and fight.

When Martin was given a loaded burp gun—a Soviet submachine gun with a round magazine below the barrel—he looked a little intimidated and awkward.

"Don't worry," said a partisan named Cesar. "After

I'm done training you, you will kill many Nazis with that weapon."

Cesar was a tall, red-faced Russian, one of six persons, including Vorobiov, who had parachuted into the Slovakian mountains to help start this particular partisan group. As second in command, Cesar was in charge of training partisans in military matters. One of the original six members was a young woman named Valesia, who handled radio repair and communications with partisan headquarters in Kiev, Russia. Another original member was 17-year-old Vanka, who was out for revenge after his father, a partisan, was killed by the Germans in Ukraine.

The day after Martin officially joined the partisans, Cesar took him to a clearing and told him to shoot the burp gun at a dead tree about 20 yards away. *This will be easy,* Martin thought. Following Cesar's directions, he raised the weapon to shoulder level, kept his head away from the barrel, aimed for the tree, and squeezed the trigger. In a two-second burst, in which he fired about 40 rounds, he lost control of the weapon, and the angle of the barrel kept rising.

Cesar laughed and said, "You have killed the tree and probably many birds."

Although Martin could barely hear because his ears were ringing from the loud noise of the burp gun, he felt good. For the first time since the war began, he possessed a sense of power and courage—and a willingness to sacrifice his life for a just cause.

The Germans had underestimated the strength of the partisan units in Czechoslovakia. Resistance to the Nazi-supporting government and the German army was growing rapidly as the number of partisans soared into the thousands. Ambushes were a favorite tactic, because the partisans couldn't openly fight the much stronger and better-equipped German army.

Captain Vorobiov's forces concentrated on mining roads and bridges and observing the movements of the enemy. To Martin, who was assigned to several scouting missions, it felt good to be a free person with a gun in his hand and revenge in his heart. All he could think about was vengeance against the Nazis for destroying his family and his youth. He wished he could talk openly to his fellow partisans about his feelings and his past, but he didn't dare because of rampant anti-Semitism.

In August 1944, the Germans were retreating on both fronts after advances by the Soviet army to the east and the Allied invasion of Nazi-occupied France to the west. Meanwhile, several large partisan groups had moved down from the mountains and occupied a 100-mile radius in the middle of Slovakia, proclaiming the area as liberated Czechoslovakia. They teamed with the deserters from the

Slovakian army to form a new unified force.

Martin's partisan unit, which had grown to 500 members, was responsible for protecting the town of Zvolen. He now was sleeping in a regular bed, eating normal food, and moving around freely. To his great joy, he learned that his brother Vilo had escaped from Sered and was also a partisan, although Martin didn't know his whereabouts.

A feeling of euphoria took hold of Martin that lifted from his heavy heart all his old miseries. *Never again will I have to fear capture by the Germans. They're too weak to try to occupy this area again.*

His unit's headquarters, a local castle, served as a center where suspicious citizens, spies, and captured German soldiers were interrogated. In one case, 20 Germans were tried and convicted by the partisans for crimes against humanity and for aiding Hitler's occupation of the country. They were sentenced to die by firing squad. On the day of execution, Martin and 14 other partisans were assigned to carry out the punishment.

When the squad arrived at the open field for the execution, the convicted Germans were digging their graves. Some were working hard, others refused to do anything, and a few cried. The defiant ones greeted the squad with shouts of "Heil Hitler!"

As Martin took his position, he thought of the suffering

of his parents, brothers, sister, and friends. This was a day he had been waiting for, a day to avenge their deaths. *Ah, revenge is going to feel so sweet! I want to see their faces when they die.*

"Ready . . . aim . . . fire!"

He pulled the trigger. And then he waited for that warm and wonderful feeling he had anticipated from getting his revenge. But, surprisingly for him, it wasn't warm and wonderful. In fact, it felt cold and terrible. Executing others couldn't bring back the dead or ease the pain in his heart. Instead, it troubled him. From then on, he was haunted by the looks on the faces of the condemned as they died.

As he grappled with his conscience, Martin was faced with other serious issues. The security enjoyed by the partisans began to crumble, because the Nazi war machine launched a major assault in Slovakia. To protect their retreat from the Russians, the Germans tried to wipe out the resistance fighters. The partisans, along with the former Slovak soldiers, formed an impressive force together during battle. But they didn't have the training or equipment to present a strong challenge against the German tanks, artillery, planes, and troop strength.

Although ammunition, food, and medical supplies were flown in from Russia, casualties for the partisans mounted into the hundreds every day. After a month of constant fighting, there was growing talk that the partisans soon would have to retreat into the mountains. As the military situation worsened, the former Slovak soldiers, who had deserted their army to join the partisans, were now deserting the partisans. Most of them threw away their uniforms and went home. *It won't be too long before I'll be on the run again,* Martin thought.

By the middle of October 1944, the Germans controlled the skies and were dropping bombs near the partisan headquarters, which was also the target of artillery shells. From desertions and casualties, the size of Captain Vorobiov's partisan group had dwindled back to its original 200 members.

As the partisans prepared to retreat, they were ordered by their commander to remove all the money from the Slovak National Bank in Zvolen so the Germans couldn't get their hands on it. Martin and his comrades carried the bags of currency from the vaults and loaded them onto trucks and wagons. Then they left the city singing partisan songs and waving good-bye to the townspeople who remained behind. Martin figured most of the citizens were relieved the partisans were leaving because that meant the Germans wouldn't subject the city to further shelling and bombing.

The convoy took two days to reach the foothills. Because the trucks couldn't go up the mountains, the partisans transferred the supplies, including the money, onto horse-drawn wagons. But days of driving rain turned the roads into muck so thick the wagons got stuck and had to be abandoned. Martin and his comrades stuffed as much money as they could in their backpacks and pockets and buried the rest. Then they continued slogging up the mountain, harassed during breaks in the weather by dive-bombing, strafing planes, and barrages of artillery shells by the Germans who had reoccupied Zvolen.

As the men climbed higher, the rain turned to snow. Temperatures fell and the winds increased. Adding to their misery, supplies were running short and their ranks were shrinking from deserters until there were only 50 remaining.

They hid by day, sleeping under the snow, and moved at night. They couldn't light fires to keep warm, because the smoke would give away their location. For four days they were without food other than instant coffee cubes and some sugar. Whenever the hunger pains became intolerable for Martin, he filled his stomach by eating snow. Like his comrades, he suffered from frozen feet and hands.

A couple of weeks earlier he couldn't imagine that the partisans would be in such bad shape. *If this is the end of my struggle for freedom, I'll die as a fighter on the battlefield and not as a victim in the gas chamber. At least I had my moment of glory as a partisan.*

The captain told the discouraged group, "The Germans have surrounded the mountain and are waiting like vultures for hunger to drive us down to face their tanks and soldiers. We can't fight them because we're nearly out of ammunition. We'll be lucky to escape. Our only chance to survive is to go back down and sneak past the Germans across the main highway."

After splitting into three groups, the partisans worked their way to the road to a spot 300 yards away from the positions of German squads on the right and the left. One by one, in the dark of night, the partisans crept across the road.

When it was Martin's turn, he made it to a ditch on the other side without being detected. But as he started climbing a steep slope, the Germans lit up the area with rocket flares and began firing. He couldn't get any traction because it was so icy. The more he kept trying to scramble up the slope, the more he kept sliding down.

Suddenly, he felt a fiery sting in his leg. "I've been shot!" he yelped. Trying not to panic, Martin searched for better footing. After several desperate attempts, he finally reached the top. Ignoring the pain, he half ran, half hobbled toward the forest, only to spot two Germans in a bunker about 400 feet away. As they raked the area with machine-gun fire, he fell to the frozen ground and crawled under the bullets until he reached cover behind several boulders. From there, he limped from rock to rock and then into the woods. After wrapping his wound to stem the bleeding, he hiked until dawn, when he rendezvoused with 30 of his comrades, including some who were bleeding badly. The other 20 partisans had either been killed or captured.

The survivors plodded on in the bitter cold and faced another mountain that they had to hike up and over. The pain in Martin's leg intensified, but there was nothing he could do about it. Too frozen in mind and body to think about food, warmth, or rest, Martin and his fellow partisans kept moving. None had the energy to talk. The silence was broken when one of the men stopped and said, "Comrades, I'm tired. I'm going to sit down for just a bit." He plopped to the ground. Within a few minutes, he was dead. The partisans buried him and continued up the other mountain until they came upon the first of several farmhouses in the area.

Because he spoke Slovak, Martin went with two other partisans to talk with the farmer. The man told them that he, his wife, and their three children had not seen any Germans. Meanwhile, outside, the other partisans found a pile of cabbage roots that the farmer had plowed up in the fall. The starving men dropped to their knees, scooped up the roots, and devoured them without bothering to clean off the dirt.

The partisans then spread out and bunked with area farmers to recuperate. Martin, who was a physical wreck, stayed with the Laska family. Totally exhausted and weak from hiking miles in the snow without food, he could hardly walk. The bullet wound in his leg had festered into a painful infection. The Laskas treated him with home remedies, shared whatever food they had, and gave him some of their sons' clothes. Within three weeks, he was back on his feet and feeling stronger. To repay the Laskas for their generosity and help, he taught their daughter math and other subjects. He also gave them some money that he had taken from the Slovak bank.

Once everyone in the group had recovered, they joined other partisans until the unit had about 100 fighters. They soon established communications with headquarters in Kiev, which arranged for nightly airdrops of supplies, including ammunition and food. Their primary function was to rebuild the group into a combat-ready unit without being seen by the Germans. Martin went on many of the daily patrols to scout and relay enemy positions and movements.

To his alarm, anti-Semitism worsened among the partisans. Nobody knew Martin was a Jew—and he intended to keep it that way. He couldn't feel safe among people who carried guns and hated Jews. Although he had good personal relationships with Captain Vorobiov and Cesar, who called Martin his best friend, he didn't trust them enough to reveal he was Jewish.

Only one partisan, a young Jew named Schwartz, let everyone know his faith. It was a fatal mistake. One day, after carrying a heavy machine gun on patrol for several hours, he asked if someone else could take it for a little while. His commander, an openly vocal anti-Semite, charged him with disobeying an order and had Schwartz executed.

Deeply shaken by the senseless death, Martin talked to Cesar about Schwartz and learned a horrible truth. "Martin, you are my friend, so I will tell you something," said Cesar. "Officially Russian laws prohibit anti-Semitism. But for myself, I hate Jews. Whenever I can, I will kill one."

To hear such hatred was a crushing disappointment for Martin, who genuinely liked Cesar. Martin said nothing. He thought, *My life is over if anyone here knows I'm Jewish.*

A few days later, a scouting patrol from another partisan group showed up. Martin recognized one of the members—Alex Engel, a fellow Jew who had been at the Sered labor camp with him. Engel ran over to Martin and whispered, "My name is Novotny, and you don't know me."

Martin replied softly, "My name is Petrasek, and you don't know me either."

Each day the dream of liberation came closer to reality. The enemy was pulling back after a series of defeats, including one in which Martin and his comrades ambushed a 100-man German patrol. Ordered to meet up with the Red Army near

Poprad 100 miles away, the partisan unit marched carefully along roads mined by the enemy.

Along the way, Martin stopped to say hello to the Laska family. It turned out to be anything but a happy reunion, because he arrived just as they were returning from a funeral. The heartbroken Laskas told him sad news—the retreating Germans had killed their son.

After offering his condolences, Martin continued on the march to Poprad, which had been liberated by the Russians. Although the war was not over, it was for these partisans. They were officially discharged, thanked for their service, and told to go home. Captain Vorobiov and Cesar were ordered to return to Russia.

As Martin said good-bye to his comrades, Cesar embraced him. "My dear friend, Martin, together we have shared starvation, freezing cold, and exhaustion. Together we have stared death in the face time and again. We have a bond between us. Let's not break it now. Come with me to Russia. There is so much we can accomplish together."

*There is absolutely no way I would go with him. Ever.* "Cesar, that sounds great," Martin lied with a straight face. "But I must return to my home. It is where I belong."

But Martin couldn't head to Bánovce yet, because it was still occupied by the Germans. He had nowhere to go. He was an 18-year-old without a home, family, money, job experience, or enough education.

Before making a decision about his future, he visited the monastery, hoping to see Brother Rudolph. But when Martin arrived, the place was deserted and in terrible condition. One of the townspeople told him, "When the Germans were retreating, they deported Prior Kostolansky, the monks, and all the inmates."

With no prospects in his future, Martin joined the Czechoslovakian army. Once again, he put himself in harm's way, dodging machine-gun fire, artillery shells, grenades, and bombs from the Germans, who still refused to surrender.

In early May 1945, the Germans made a final stand in Prague, Czechoslovakia's largest city. But the Russians routed them. By then, Martin was with a Czechoslovakian unit that was among the first to enter Prague. Flags flew, bands played, and people danced. As he and his fellow soldiers—all dirty, weary, and unshaven—drove down the main boulevard, they were greeted with flowers, kisses, food, drinks, and invitations for home-cooked meals from deliriously happy citizens of all ages.

For Martin it was an unbelievable feeling. He basked in the glory of victory, of helping free his homeland from the clutches of the enemy. He had gone from prisoner to partisan to liberator. *The war is over*, he told himself. *There's no more danger of being killed. I don't have to worry about trying to survive. Now I can think about living.*

≡

*After the war, Martin learned that his brothers Morris
and Samuel were living in Palestine (before it became
Israel), and he reunited with his brother Vilo, a fellow
partisan. Martin, who kept the name Petrasek, completed
four years of high school in eight months and then studied
civil engineering at the University of Bratislava for
three years.*

*Following the communist takeover of Czechoslovakia,
he immigrated to Israel and continued his studies at
the Technical University in Haifa, earning a degree in
engineering. For the next seven years, he supervised the
development of 17 settlements for new immigrants in
Israel.*

*Married with two children, Martin moved to the
United States in 1959 and became a citizen in 1964. He
formed his own highly successful company that develops
land and builds homes and apartment buildings. Martin,
who lives in Sherman Oaks, California, still heads the
firm.*

*"We must always remain vigilant because evil can
happen at any time," he says. "I was raised in a democratic
country, Czechoslovakia, just like America, and just
like Germany before Hitler. As the regime changed in*

*Germany, millions of Jews were killed because too many people were afraid to stand up and fight against evil. If you are in danger of persecution, you must fight for your rights by any means possible. And if you see others being persecuted, you must fight for them, too, because what happens to them could end up happening to you."*

Martin Petrasek's life story can be seen in the DVD *Broken Promise*, produced by Genta Film, and in his self-published book of the same name.

# CHONON BEDZOWSKI

SEVENTEEN-YEAR-OLD CHONON Bedzowski, his mother, and three siblings had just finished sitting *Shiva*—the Jewish seven-day period of ritual mourning—for his father, Michael, in their home in Lida, Belorussia (now Belarus).

Michael, who had owned a department store, had passed away from a failing kidney, devastating Chonon; his brother, Benny, 9; his sisters, Leah, 18, and Sonia, 16; and his mother, Chasia. Since the Soviets had taken over the city two years earlier, in 1939, the Bedzowskis' once comfy life had become much more difficult. The new government had forced Michael to give up ownership of his store, rationed food, and left the family in near poverty. Now he was gone.

*Can things get any worse?* Chonon wondered. His answer came shortly after sitting *Shiva*, on June 22, 1941. Suddenly squadrons of Luftwaffe planes darkened the skies over Lida and dropped hundreds of incendiary bombs that torched the city from one end to the other.

Chonon and his family gathered what few belongings they could and fled into streets of chaos. As fires raged and buildings exploded, panic-stricken refugees screamed and wailed in their mad rush from the advancing German army. Enemy fighter planes roared low and strafed roads clogged with people, cars, buses, and horse-drawn wagons along with retreating Russian tanks, trucks, and soldiers.

During the Bedzowskis' harried run to an outlying village, Chonon saw abandoned, bullet-riddled vehicles and bodies strewn on the side of the road. Over the next few weeks, the family found shelter in the barns of kindhearted gentile farmers. But once the Germans took control of Lida, they ordered all Jews in the area to return to the city. Failure to comply was punishable by death to the Jews and to those who were protecting them. Fearing for their own safety, the farmers no longer were willing to hide the family.

So the Bedzowskis went back to their ruined city. From the moment the Germans occupied Lida, terror, brutality, and bloodshed became a way of life for the Jews. All males between the ages of 15 and 60, which included Chonon, were taken under armed guard every day to perform hard labor, mostly clearing away the rubble from the bombed-out buildings. Any slackers were shot to death or whipped mercilessly. Soon all females between 16 and 40 were required to serve in the Nazi cause. All the Bedzowskis, except Benny, were part of a strenuous, exhausting work detail that unloaded coal and ammunition from trains.

Chonon and his family grew increasingly weak from lack of food. Their main nourishment from the Nazis was one bowl each of soup made from rotten potatoes. Any Jew caught with butter, meat, or eggs was shot on the spot. But that didn't stop Leah from sneaking out past curfew at night to beg or trade for food from nearby farmers.

Most every day, the workers were bullied and beaten. Throughout the winter, one sadistic Nazi officer, Rudolph Werner, rode around in his sleigh armed with a shotgun and a horsewhip, which he used to harass the laborers. He also would sic a ferocious German shepherd named Donner (German for *thunder*) on Jews for his amusement.

By spring 1942, Chonon and his family were hearing rumors that the Nazis were plotting the slaughter of Lida's Jews. Throughout the occupation, he knew that Germans were always finding excuses to murder groups of Jews, but up until then the city hadn't been the site for such wholesale killings.

That changed on May 8. Before dawn, the Bedzowskis were rousted out of bed. Nazi commandos, in teams of 10 to 12 men, surrounded the Jewish sections of the city and ordered everyone outside. Those who didn't move fast enough were dragged out of their homes and beaten.

Chonon and his family were pushed into the street, which was crowded with frightened people in their nightgowns and pajamas. As the 7,500 Jews were marched to central locations, he wondered, *Will this be the last day of my life?*

"Form up in lines, family by family!" shouted an officer. "Have your papers ready!"

Chonon looked around at the trembling, fearful masses. An occasional shot rang out followed by a scream. He knew somewhere in the crowd a person's loved one had just been executed, probably for being too slow or for saying the wrong thing.

As he stood in line, he saw a Nazi officer telling people in front of him to gather either to the left or to the right. He noticed that skilled workers were generally directed to the left while nearly everyone else—the young, old, and unfit—was ordered to the right. *The ones on the right, are they going to be killed?* he wondered.

When the Bedzowskis reached the front of the line, the officer checked their papers and stared each one in the eye. *Which way is he going to point?* Chonon thought, holding his breath. The unsmiling officer flicked his thumb to the left for Chonon, his sisters, and mother. But Benny was ordered to the right.

Chonon reached out to grab his little brother, but it

was no use. He was shoved off to the other group. Fraught with worry over Benny's fate, the family was relieved when minutes later he crawled away undetected from the group on the right and rejoined his mother and siblings.

Those on the left were told to go home. Those on the right—about 5,500 men, women, and children—were marched to the edge of the city. By 5 P.M. the last of them had been machine-gunned by a death squad of 100 bloodthirsty gunmen.

These execution commandos then traveled to nearby towns and massacred thousands more. Meanwhile, the remaining Jews in the city and other nearby towns were herded into a ghetto in Lida surrounded by barbed wire. For days, Chonon could hear the weeping of survivors who lost loved ones and were reciting Kaddish for the dead.

Chonon, like so many other trapped young Jews, realized that there was no point remaining in the ghetto, awaiting his turn to die. He wanted to escape into the nearby forest to the partisans whose exploits of ambushes and sabotage gave him a glimmer of hope.

Of special interest was the partisan unit headed by three tall, brawny Jewish brothers, Tuvia, Asael, and Zus Bielski, who were acquaintances of the Bedzowskis. The brothers had helped run the family farm and mill until the Germans invaded the region. After the murders of the brothers' parents, two younger siblings, Tuvia's wife, and Zus's wife and baby daughter, the trio sought refuge in the woods where they formed their own small military organization.

A former soldier in the Polish army, Tuvia was the leader of a unit that, unlike most any other partisan group, was willing to accept any Jew—young or old, armed or unarmed, sick or healthy. It started out with 20 relatives and close friends, but its membership grew as they helped others escape from nearby ghettos. Although its ranks were growing with unarmed people, the group included several dedicated fighters who engaged in hit-and-run attacks on local Nazis and collaborators.

But many people were reluctant to leave the ghetto after getting assurances from German officials that the mass killings were over and that as long as they continued to work hard, the remaining Jews had nothing to worry about. Another reason many chose to stay was the belief that if they escaped, they would freeze to death in the forest or would be found by the Nazis and executed.

"Even a winter in the forest is better than another day in the ghetto," Chonon said to those who didn't want to leave.

At the beginning of 1943, the Nazis distributed leaflets to the Christian population warning that Tuvia and his men were dangerous and were avenging the murders of Jews. The leaflet offered a reward of 50,000 German marks (later doubled) for information that would lead to his capture.

A short while later, Konstanty Kozlowski, a gentile friend of Tuvia's, delivered a note to the Bedzowskis that would change their lives. It was from Tuvia, urging the family to escape before all the Jews were liquidated. The note explained that Kozlowski was a trusted friend of the Bielskis and would help the Bedzowskis.

As a gentile, he was able to move around freely and made his living traveling the countryside selling cheap merchandise from his horse-drawn cart. The Nazis ignored the unassuming, quiet man and never considered he was secretly helping the Jews, especially because his brother was a policeman who worked with the Germans.

On a frigid night in February 1943, Kozlowski led Chonon and his family out of their home. Slowly and quietly, they crept their way through the deserted ghetto streets before dropping to their stomachs and crawling up to a barbed wire fence. No one said a word, fearing that any sound would alert the vicious guard dogs that patrolled the perimeter. Kozlowski dug a small hole, allowing the Bedzowskis to slide under the cold wire meshing one by one. Once everyone had wriggled through, Kozlowski packed the dirt back into the hole so the ghetto guards wouldn't notice anything amiss. The Bedzowskis continued on their hands and knees across a field. Once they reached a wooded area,

Kozlowski declared, "You are going to live."

They hiked in the countryside for the next two days to the Bielski camp located in a dense forest. When he arrived, Chonon was astonished by what he saw. It wasn't so much the rough-looking men cleaning their weapons, or the young people tending to a roaring fire, or the women making soup over a large kettle. No, what truly awed him was seeing so many Jews—there were about 300 of them by now—doing these chores without being held captive by the Nazis. *This must be one of the few places in all of Europe where Jews can move around in total freedom,* Chonon thought. For the first time in years, the teenager felt free.

As he always did, Tuvia greeted the new arrivals. The 36-year-old broad-shouldered leader had arrived on a white horse accompanied by several other mounted partisans, including his two brothers, Asael, 34, who was second in command, and Zus, 30, the lead scout and intelligence gatherer. Clad in a long leather jacket, knee-high boots, and a military hat, Tuvia had a machine gun strapped across his chest. To Chonon, Tuvia looked like the biggest hero in the world.

Tuvia took off his right glove and shook hands with each member of the Bedzowski family before turning to introduce his two younger brothers. He explained that the main goal of his partisan unit was to rescue Jews like themselves. "I would rather save one old Jewish woman than kill ten Nazis," he said. But, he added, the partisans were also seeking vengeance against the Nazis for all the Jewish blood that had been spilled. "The world should know there are still Jews alive, especially Jewish partisans willing to fight."

He explained that everyone in camp, no matter how strong or weak, could contribute to the general well-being of the others—and all had to follow his rules.

Within a few weeks, Chonon realized that although Tuvia projected an air of fearlessness, confidence, and firmness, he was also a man of great compassion. Many times he tenderly hugged a child or an elderly person and openly wept when hearing a heart-wrenching story of the suffering a new arrival endured in the ghetto. Tuvia always made time to ask about each person's health.

The Bedzowskis came during a period when the Bielski Brigade was growing significantly larger. As Tuvia explained to them, "The war is starting to go against the Nazis, so the killing of Jews is becoming a top priority. The Germans are even taking away trains needed by their own soldiers and using them to transport more Jews to the gas chambers."

To accommodate the new arrivals, the partisans built more wood and earthen dugouts that were cleverly camouflaged with trees, bushes, and ground cover. Near each hidden structure was a campfire for staying warm and cooking food.

Like his comrades, Chonon ate mostly potatoes that were baked directly on the coals. Large tubs retrieved from nearby villages were used for bathing, laundering, and cooking.

By spring 1943, the Bielski Brigade had 400 members, including 100 fighters. Many newcomers had escaped from ghettos, work camps, and concentration camps and had walked for days in the Nazi-infested countryside to find the Jewish partisans. Every time someone new entered the camp, it represented another small victory—and fueled outrage among the enemy.

The camp's armed men were reorganized into fighting squads of eight to ten persons. In addition to ambushing enemy supply trucks, they burned wooden bridges and chopped down telephone and telegraph poles. Chonon was assigned to one of the teams in charge of collecting food and supplies for the group. Other squads were formed to free those still imprisoned in the ghettos, especially the 2,000 remaining Jews in Lida. Often a few of Tuvia's men would sneak at night into the city's brewery, which was staffed by several Jews who were allowed to live there. The next morning, the partisans would put on clothes with yellow stars, pretending to be one of the ghetto dwellers. Then they would gather a small group of Jews and help them escape.

Since joining the partisans, the Bedzowskis had reached a level of comfort and security that they hadn't felt in years.

But Chonon and his sisters, Leah and Sonia, still went on dangerous missions. Benny was too young yet, so he stayed behind to gather firewood and help their mother, Chasia.

With the growing number of refugees showing up at the camp, food and medicine were always in short supply. Sonia sneaked back into Lida numerous times to obtain certain medicines and medical supplies. But on one such mission, she never returned. To the horror of the family, they learned she had been captured and transported to a death camp, where she was murdered.

By June, the population of the Bielski Brigade had swelled to 700, which heartened the partisans, but its size was also putting them in peril. The Germans knew where they were in the Stara-Huta woods and sent a plane to strafe the camp. It was obvious to Tuvia and his brothers that it was time to move. He gathered everyone and said, "I can't promise anything. We could live a day. We could live longer. But we have to go to a different forest, because they have found out we are here. We don't have to be heroes. We just have to live through this war." As tears welled up in his eyes, he added, "Whoever will make it, he is the biggest hero."

The Bedzowskis packed up everything they could and helped load horse-drawn carts and wagons. As cows ambled alongside them, the partisans headed out in single file in a line that stretched for more than a half mile. That evening they settled in a poplar forest and set up kitchens and temporary shelters.

A few nights later, Chonon was chatting with his family when Asael rode in on his horse, shouting, "The Germans are coming! The Germans are coming!"

Amid shrieks of terror, women and children abandoned their shelters, knocking over cookware and other supplies, and leaving behind the livestock as they fled deeper into the forest. Meanwhile, Chonon and the fighters grabbed their weapons to patrol the area and mount a defense.

The rumbling of the German trucks grew louder until the din was drowned out by the barrage of machine-gun fire and mortar shells. Seeing the muzzle flashes from enemy weapons, Chonon estimated there were at least 100 German soldiers advancing toward the camp. *There's no way we can hold them off,* he thought.

"Everyone must retreat!" Asael shouted. "Get out of here now!"

Chonon and his comrades dashed farther into the forest and fortunately were not pursued by the Germans. When everyone regrouped, they discovered that six men had been killed and four others—three women and a child—had been wounded.

Weeks later, the partisans received word that the Germans were preparing to launch "Operation Hermann"—a vast military operation aimed at annihilating all the villages and settlements in the area as well as the Russian, Polish, and Jewish partisans. An estimated 50,000 troops planned to surround the huge forest, block all escape routes, and force the partisans into their only option—death. The Jews called it the Big Hunt.

Once again Tuvia spoke in front of all his people. "Such a large group can't stay here. We've learned the German army is bringing reinforcements to fight the partisans. Soon they will be searching for us. So we have decided to move to the Naliboki Puscha. Reaching these great woods will be a perilous journey across enemy territory. But it's our best chance of surviving, because the forest is large and the swamps are deep. We will seek refuge on a large island called Krasnaya Gorka. During our journey we must maintain absolute silence, and everyone must obey orders. Leave all unimportant things behind. Take as much food as you can carry. Remain courageous and quiet until the danger passes."

Like most everyone else, Chonon felt a sense of doom about embarking on a treacherous 24-mile journey to the Naliboki Puscha, a thick pine forest in northwestern Belorussia. It meant leaving the small forest that had been the only home he had known since escaping from the ghetto. He had become familiar with the landscape and the peasants who had provided food to the partisans.

That night Chonon, Leah, Benny, and Chasia packed what little food they had left and joined the lengthy procession of 800 souls on a hazardous march to a place that would be difficult to get to and difficult to live in. Because everyone needed to travel as lightly as possible, they left behind most of their supplies and their horses and livestock. Walking in single file to minimize the footprints, those who carried children were at the front while the armed fighters took up the rear. No one spoke or made any noise, not even the children. The only sounds Chonon heard were the squishing of feet in the muck and the howling of wolves. At times he sank up to his chest in the swampy water, but he and the others slogged on for hours until they reached a dry area. Exhausted, many fell asleep. Anyone who snored was awakened to maintain strict silence.

Around midnight, Chonon and his comrades were startled by a booming voice coming from a distant loudspeaker: "Partisans, you know you cannot fight a war against our tanks and cannons. When daylight comes, throw down your guns and surrender!"

At dawn, the Germans began launching mortar shells, prompting people to flee in all directions. Fortunately, the area was overgrown with tall grasses and provided cover so the Luftwaffe planes circling above couldn't spot them.

In the confusion, the Bedzowskis became lost. Afraid

to holler to the others for fear it would give their location away to the enemy, the family huddled by a tree and tried to figure out what to do next. In the distance, they could hear German shepherds barking and Nazi soldiers and collaborators shouting encouragement to one another to keep hunting for the partisans. Sporadic gunfire rang out. As the stalking enemy drew closer, the Bedzowskis reached a critical emotional point: They didn't expect to live; they just didn't want to be captured.

But then they were blessed with a lucky break. A Russian-born partisan, Wolf "The Machine Gunner" Janson had been assigned by Tuvia to look for lost people. During his search, he stumbled upon the wayward family and guided them back to the brigade. Once everyone was gathered, they continued their slow, agonizing march, trudging through the muck, mud, and water night after night. Overhead, enemy planes circled like buzzards in search of the well-hidden partisans. Despite being soaked, filthy, fatigued, and terribly hungry, everyone remained resolute. When it was time to rest in the swamp, many dozed off in trees or slept after strapping themselves to tree trunks so they wouldn't slip into the murky water.

They finally arrived at the island of Krasnaya Gorka, but it was hardly a haven. Because the Germans were only a few miles away, the partisans couldn't go far to gather food.

And even if they could, they wouldn't find much because the nearby settlements had been destroyed. The partisans had to sit tight while mortar rounds and bombs pounded the area. As the days passed, the food dilemma grew worse and some people began showing signs of starvation.

The relentless German attack thundered on for an unbearable week, wearing down the people's will. Some started to lose hope, wondering if this would be their final resting place. *Either we leave soon or we die,* Chonon thought.

Out of options, Tuvia made a difficult, but necessary, decision. Following his orders, the partisans broke up into small groups of 20 to 30 and headed back through the swamps to the very forest from which they had come—the place that had been considered too unsafe for them to live. Miraculously, they slipped past the German ring of terror. Eight hundred starving, exhausted partisans, who had spent two harrowing weeks dodging a fearsome force that had them completely surrounded, had just pulled off one of the war's greatest escapes.

But the triumph was muted when the partisans learned that the Germans had wiped out every village and settlement in the Naliboki Puscha, murdered thousands of peasants there, and transported thousands more to slave labor camps in Germany.

Life over the next month didn't get much easier for the

partisans. The Soviet military, which controlled most of the partisan groups, ordered the Bielski Brigade split into two sections—one for the 200 fighters, with Zus as deputy commander, and the other for unarmed men, women, and children, led by Tuvia. Asael was assigned to another partisan unit. The change meant that Zus's group would fight with Soviet partisans while Tuvia's people would head back to, of all places, the heart of the Naliboki Puscha.

After a risky and weary summer of eluding the Germans, the people were being told to reenter an enormous kill-zone. Nearly 100 Bielski fighters defied the Soviets' order and remained with Tuvia to help protect the remaining 600 partisans. So once again Chonon and his comrades trudged back through the marshes and swamps to the Naliboki Puscha. Meanwhile, on September 17, the Germans sent the remaining 2,000 Jews in the Lida ghetto to the gas chambers at Majdanek, a Polish extermination camp.

After the Bielski Brigade arrived safely in the Naliboki Puscha, members set up camp in a dense area so they couldn't be spotted by the Luftwaffe. Then the Jews went to work, turning it into a thriving settlement—the very kind that the Germans had been destroying throughout the region. It would be called Jerusalem.

Chonon and his family helped build dugouts that accommodated 50 people each. After rummaging through the ruins of nearby burned-out villages, the partisans retrieved blacksmith anvils, sewing machines, a meat grinder, and other equipment. Before long, the village had a sausage-making building and a smokehouse operated by two kosher butchers. A small horse-powered mill ground wheat and other grains to make flour that was used by the bakery to make bread.

The partisans built workshops with high ceilings, large windows, and wood-burning stoves. Eighteen tailors patched up torn clothes and stitched together new garments from discarded shirts and pants. A tannery produced the leather and hide for the two dozen shoemakers who repaired and made shoes and boots while leather workers fashioned bridles, saddles, holsters, and ammunition belts. Loggers cut down trees, which the carpenters used to create tables and rifle stocks. Metalworkers repaired damaged weapons and built new ones out of old parts, while blacksmiths shoed horses for the group's 30 mounted partisans. Also practicing their pre-war craft were watchmakers, hatmakers, and three barbers. Young people did their part by gathering wood, tending to fires, and looking after the herd of 60 cows that provided milk.

The village had two separate medical facilities—a clinic for the sick and wounded and a quarantine hut for those suffering from deadly, infectious typhus. There was even a dentist on call. But medical supplies were extremely limited, so the partisans relied on folk remedies and naturally grown medications. They also built a bathhouse where people poured water over heated stones to create steam, which eased aching muscles and helped rid their bodies of lice.

To keep children busy and out of trouble, two teachers taught them basic subjects and led them in songs and games. As a break from the day-to-day work, a professional ballet dancer formed an entertainment troupe that held variety shows featuring folk dances, popular songs, and skits.

The settlement also had a jail, which was a dark, unventilated dugout watched over by an armed guard. A lawyer among the partisans acted as a judge and jury in cases where someone violated the rules.

For the Bedzowskis and others, the fear of being attacked slowly diminished and was replaced by a sense of normalcy that had been dormant for years. Even love was in the air. Leah gave her heart to Wolf Janson, the Soviet partisan who had rescued the family when they were lost. The couple was wed in the woods in front of their comrades.

Part of the feeling of security came from knowing that the many Soviet partisan units in the forest were close enough to provide protection. But there were still dangers for Chonon, who often went out on sabotage, scouting, and ambush missions like the one on January 28, 1944, when the partisans set up one of their more elaborate traps.

Upon entering the village of Vasilevitch, ten Jewish partisans pretended to be drunk by guzzling from vodka bottles that contained only water. They shouted, cursed, and shot their pistols into the air, annoying the peasants until one of them ran off to a nearby outpost and alerted the Germans. Meanwhile, more than 150 partisans, including Chonon, surrounded the village without being seen.

Less than an hour later, a convoy of 26 policemen and 8 Nazi officers roared into town. On a prearranged signal—a whistle—the partisans attacked. During the deadly firefight, the Jews killed 30 men, including all the officers. The partisans lost 4 men and had 3 others wounded. Although he was shot at many times, Chonon wasn't hit. But he came close to being struck. He discovered a hole in his pants from a bullet that narrowly missed his leg.

Throughout the winter, Jewish refugees continued to trickle into the bustling Bielski village. Chonon always got a warm feeling whenever he saw their look of wonder upon entering the camp of the largest gathering of free Jews in the region. He remembered how thunderstruck and relieved he was when he first arrived. Now every time he returned from a mission, he felt pride over what he and his comrades had created by relying on their courage, resourcefulness, and sweat.

On May 1, 1944, everyone in the Bielski Brigade gathered for a May Day celebration in the center of the settlement, which was adorned, for the day, with red flags. Standing alongside commanders of other nearby partisan units, Tuvia announced that the Red Army had the Germans on the run. "The war will soon reach the German heartland, and there the Nazi monster will finally be crushed!" he bellowed to the cheers of his fellow partisans. "But the front is rapidly approaching us, so we can expect difficult days ahead when the retreating Germans come through this area. We must be ready . . . and we will. Victory is clearly before us!"

Early on the morning of July 9, a force of 200 retreating German soldiers sneaked past partisan guard posts and charged toward the Bielski camp. Before the partisans could mount a strong defense, the Germans poured into the camp, spraying bullets into workshops and tossing grenades into dugouts. They also scrounged for food because they hadn't eaten in days. Hundreds of unarmed men, women, and children scattered into the woods and marshes to hide while their armed comrades launched a counterattack. But the outmanned partisan fighters were driven back.

Hearing the sounds of battle, nearby partisan units raced to the settlement and helped rout the Germans. When the fighting was over, nine members of the Bielski Brigade had been killed and two dozen wounded. As depressing as it was, the day ended on a positive note. News reached the camp that the Red Army had overrun the Germans and was just a few miles away.

Shortly after the partisans buried their dead, a steady procession of young Soviet soldiers marched past them in triumph and shouted, "You can go home! Your war is over!"

Chonon and his family embraced and wept. His brother-in-law, Wolf Janson, joyously yelled, "After so many years, we are finally free!"

Through his tear-filled eyes, Chonon tried to soak in this incredibly happy and stirring moment. He had been part of something historic and extraordinary. This band of strong-willed Jews—a group that began as a small gathering of Bielski relatives and had grown to more than 1,200—had survived in the woods against a ruthless and powerful enemy that had slaughtered millions. They had endured so much—moving from place to place, hiding in swamps for days, trekking endlessly through dangerous territory, eluding German soldiers and their henchmen, and dodging bullets and bombs. And yet out of all the adversity and peril, out of all the mayhem and madness, these partisans had created their own haven in the forest—a remarkable testament to their courage and fortitude.

The day after they were liberated, Tuvia summoned everyone to the center of their settlement and gave his final speech to his people: "My dear brothers and sisters, we have suffered through very hard times together. We have been attacked and blockaded. We have been cold and hungry. We have been in constant fear of our lives. Now we are going to tell the world that we, a tiny remnant of a people, had been struggling to save ourselves and our tortured brethren. We are witnesses to what Hitler and his killers have done. We will bear witness to the murder and destruction, to the suffering that the Nazis brought upon the Jewish people."

For Chonon, their survival held further significance. As he repeatedly said, "We are the Jewish brigade that the Germans could never destroy!"

≡

*When the Bielski Brigade was dismissed, it officially had 1,230 members, making it the largest Jewish partisan unit—as well as rescue of Jews by Jews—in all of Nazi-occupied Europe. By all accounts, it was one of the most noteworthy Jewish resistance efforts of World War II.*

*Chonon and his family returned to Lida, where they lived for eight months. They eventually made their way through Poland, Czechoslovakia, Hungary, and Austria until they ended up in a displaced persons camp in Torino, Italy. There, he married Sara Golcman, a Polish-born partisan, in 1946.*

*In 1949 the entire family immigrated to Montreal,*

Canada, where he westernized his name to Charles Bedzow. He opened wholesale and retail businesses that sold imported furniture and jewelry. Then he launched a highly successful international real estate company that develops property for residential and commercial use and owns several major office buildings. Charles and Sara, who live in Montreal and are Canadian citizens, raised three children. Chasia lived with them until her death in 2000. The couple has been involved in raising money for Jewish schools, universities, and hospitals in Canada, the United States, and Israel.

In 2011, Charles was named honorary international chairman of the Jewish Partisans Educational Foundation. He accepted the honor at a JPEF tribute dinner celebrating the Jewish partisans' legacy. At the special event, attended by 55 survivors and 350 family and friends, Charles was introduced by his granddaughter, Lauren Feingold, the youngest member on JPEF's board.

Leah and Wolf, whose last name was changed to Johnson, raised three children in Montreal. After Wolf's death in 1979, Leah moved to Hallandale, Florida, and spends her free time giving talks about her experiences as a partisan to synagogues and Jewish organizations.

Benny, who westernized his name to Benjamin Bedzow, became a successful real estate developer. He and his wife, Bessie, raised three children and live in Miami.

*After leaving the forest, Asael Bielski was drafted into the Red Army and was killed in combat several months later in Germany. Tuvia and Zus immigrated to Israel where they each married and had three children. Both families moved to Brooklyn, New York, in 1956 and lived quiet lives in the Jewish community, which knew all about their heroic deeds, but the rest of the world didn't.*

*In 1986, Charles was the international chairman of a celebration in New York, sponsored by Touro College, honoring Tuvia, on his eightieth birthday, and the Bielski Brigade. Tuvia died a year later. Zus died in 1995.*

*It is because the members of the Bielski Brigade resisted the Nazis and survived the Holocaust that an estimated 20,000 people, who otherwise would not have been born, exist today—their children, grandchildren, and great-grandchildren.*

You can learn more about the Bielski Brigade in the books *The Bielski Brothers* by Peter Duffy (Harper Perennial), *Fugitives of the Forest* by Allan Levin (Lyons Press), and *Defiance: The Bielski Partisans* by Nechama Tec (Oxford University Press). The true story is also told in the feature film *Defiance*, starring Daniel Craig, and in the History Channel documentary *The Bielski Brothers: Jerusalem in the Woods*.

# ABOUT THE AUTHOR

ALLAN ZULLO is the author of more than 100 nonfiction books on subjects ranging from sports and the supernatural to history and animals.

He has introduced Scholastic readers to the Ten True Tales series, gripping stories of extraordinary persons— many of them young people—who have met the challenges of dangerous, sometimes life-threatening, situations. Among the books in the series are *World War II Heroes*, *Heroes of 9/11*, and *Titanic: Young Survivors*. In addition, he has authored three other books about the real-life experiences of young people during the Holocaust—*Survivors: True Stories of Children in the Holocaust*, *Heroes of the Holocaust: True Stories of Rescues by Teens*, and *Escape: Children of the Holocaust*.

Allan, the grandfather of five and the father of two grown daughters, lives with his wife, Kathryn, on the side of a mountain near Asheville, North Carolina. To learn more about the author, visit his website at www.allanzullo.com.